THE
IMPERIAL AGE
OF VENICE
1380—1580

THE IMPERIAL AGE OF VENICE

1380–1580

D. S. CHAMBERS

with 131 illustrations, 20 in colour

THAMES AND HUDSON · LONDON

1 *Frontispiece*
A climax in imperial imagery:
Veronese's *Apotheosis of Venice* (*c.* 1583) on
the ceiling of the hall of the greater council.

Printed and bound in Great Britain by Jarrold and Sons Ltd Norwich

ISBN 0 500 32020 9 CLOTHBOUND
ISBN 0 500 33020 4 PAPERBOUND

CONTENTS

PREFACE

I owe a great debt to those who have helped in the preparation of this book. In the first place I am grateful to Professor Lionel Butler who encouraged me to write it and suggested ways of improving it, and to Mr Douglas Johnson who thought of the title. I have benefited greatly from the comments of Professor John Steer, Dr Jonathan Riley-Smith, Mr Richard de Lavigne, Dr Cecil Clough and Miss Jaynie Anderson; also from the editorial suggestions of Professor Geoffrey Barraclough, Mr Stanley Baron and Mr Jamie Camplin. Mr Antonio Montalto, himself a Venetian patriot, took much care over finding the illustrations. I am also grateful to the University of St Andrews for grants from its Travel and Research Funds. Finally I owe most thanks to my Mother, who read the roughest drafts and encouraged me to finish the book at a difficult time.

2 The lion of St Mark by Carpaccio.

INTRODUCTION

Among the cities of medieval Italy which attained not only an Italian but a European importance, Jacob Burkhardt distinguished Florence and Venice as having a 'deep significance for the human race'. For Florence, this dictum has become well established, on the strength of Florentine art, literature, political ideas, industry, institutional development and social change. For Venice, which evolved very differently, it deserves new emphasis and illustration.

This book investigates Venice during the two centuries after 1380. It is not solely concerned with political and economic power but with all the attributes of Venetian society and civilization during this 'Imperial Age', which saw a summit of Venetian prosperity in the early fifteenth century and a great expansion of Venetian dominion both overseas and in Italy: when Venice's success and survival aroused widespread fear, then reverence.

Although commerce is not the main subject of the book, it must be stressed that this was the principal source of Venetian power in the Mediterranean world. Trade and urban life in Italy were already reviving by the early ninth century and grew with great impetus from the eleventh century onwards; in this resurgence, the group of lagoon-bound sandbanks at the head of the Adriatic Sea was well situated to become a great port.

Naturally defensible, and accessible from the great plain of north-east Italy between the Apennines and the Julian Alps, it became the successor to the late Roman ports of Aquileia and Ravenna. The local transport of salt, corn, timber, wine and other necessities along the coasts of the Adriatic and up the rivers of the plain was, and remained, a fundamental source of wealth; but the site also had special opportunities for developing long-distance trade. Political association with the Byzantine empire first helped it to become a leading western emporium for spices, the trade description given not only to flavourings such as pepper and ginger, but to all manner of goods from cotton and mineral dyes to peacocks' feathers, brought from Constantinople, Alexandria and other eastern ports, Moslem as well as Christian. Accessibility from the Germanic centre of Europe, through the eastern passes over the Alps and down the rivers Adige, Piave, Brenta or Tagliamento, made it a market of more than Italian importance. The mineral wealth of Tyrol, Styria, Carinthia and beyond – silver, copper, iron and other metals – was brought to or through Venice where German merchants sought Mediterranean goods in exchange.

Great emphasis must be placed upon the Byzantine connection, for it had a permanent relevance to Venetian history shared by no other Italian city. After the sixth-century conquests of Justinian, the lagoon region had passed under the rule of the exarch of Ravenna; it had its own military magistrates but they were subject to imperial authority. The iconoclast troubles of the empire seem to have coincided with a rebellion; Orso, the military leader elected in 726, is now regarded as the forerunner of the independent dukes or 'doges'. The fall of Ravenna to the Lombards in 751, and the pact between the eastern and western empires in 814, left the lagoon community in an enviable position. The island of Rialto became the Venetians' capital; there, virtually autonomous under their elected doges and increasingly Latinized, they continued to benefit from the Byzantine connection. Doge Orseolo's expedition against the Dalmatian ports in 1000 recovered for Venice the lost Byzantine authority on that coast; in 1082, Venetian help to the empire against the Normans, who were conquering southern Italy and striking ambitiously across the Adriatic, brought preference and customs exemptions in Byzantine ports.

During the twelfth century, however, relations changed. The First Crusade, which succeeded in capturing Jerusalem

(1099), was not aided by Venice, but by the Pisans and Genoese, who had a long experience of conflict with Moslems in the western Mediterranean. Nevertheless, Venetian interests could not ignore the trading opportunities in the new kingdom of Jerusalem, even if its foundation was an embarrassment to the empire. Venetian naval support was sent against Jaffa in 1100, and was largely responsible for the capture of Tyre (1124) from the Fatimids of Egypt. Extensive concessions were granted to Venice for trade and settlement in the Syrian ports. On the other hand, Italian rivals were also receiving privileges in Constantinople, and Byzantine relations with Venice deteriorated. The Venetian fleet had attacked Corfu in the winter of 1122–23; war broke out again in 1171–72; in 1204 came the momentous sequel when doge Enrico Dandolo, who had provided transport for the Fourth Crusade, took a leading part in the capture of Constantinople and acquired for Venice trading advantages (including access to the Black Sea), maritime possessions and prestige far exceeding those of any other Italian port. Yet if political circumstances changed, the eastern interest of Venice remained constant; the restoration of a Greek emperor at Constantinople in 1261, and the Moslem reconquest of Syria, completed with the capture of Acre in 1291, brought reorganization, but business continued without any long-lasting interruption.

The prosperity of Venice as a maritime power and trading emporium – Martino da Canale wrote (c. 1267–75) 'merchandise passes through this noble city as water flows through fountains' – depended not only upon its location and eastern connections but also, of course, upon certain material and human resources. Among these were the abundant supplies of timber and other materials for shipbuilding obtained from the Alpine foothills and Istria; manpower, skilled and unskilled; merchant patricians who were astute and literate in their methods of business, navigation and administration, ready to spread their risks, reinvest their profits and investigate new opportunities in all directions.

9

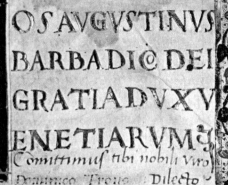

NOS AVGVSTINVS BARBADICO DEI GRATIA DVX VENETIARVM &

Comittimus tibi nobili viro
Dominico Trono Dilecto
Ciui et fideli nostro q̃ in nomine Jesu christi et in
bona gratia uadas Potestas loci nostri Este in quo
regimine stare et esse debeas p̃ unum annum co
tinuu a die qua applicueris & tantum plus q̃ tui
successor tuus illuc uenire distulerit Quam terre
cum locis et uillis ad ipsam p̃tinentibus et specta
tibus ac Homines in ea exystentibus regere & gube
nare debeas & Ratione & iustitiam face inter eos
in ciuilibus et Criminalibus secundum Consuetudiez
dicte terre Obsuabis statuta Ciuitatis nostre Padu
que facient ad tuum Regimen saluo semp Arbitrio
nostri domini addẽ minuere ac corrigẽ ad bene
placitum nostri Diem aut Qua regimen applicu
eris nobis tuis litteris denotabis
HAbere Quidẽ debes pro salario tuo libras Mille qua
dringentas p̃ in anno et ratione anni Tenendo in tuo
Regimine ad tuum salarium & expens duos famlos

4 St Mark's, a primary symbol of Venetian glory.

No city is exactly comparable to another, and least of all perhaps can a parallel be found for Venice. Among other maritime cities of Italy, the situations and the internal and external developments of Pisa and Genoa were, for instance, very different. Pisa, gradually silting up, had easy access only to the valley of the river Arno; Genoa, the rival which superseded Pisa in the thirteenth century, was built precariously upon the Alpine fringe, and had access to Lombardy only through a mountain pass. The later rival of Venice as leading Italian republic, Florence, was an inland manufacturing and financial centre which grew up in the thirteenth century. Not these, but Rome itself, was taken by many contemporaries as the city most worthy to provide a parallel with Venice at its zenith; and the false analogy provides a theme with which this book will be much concerned.

◀ 3 Commission from doge Agostino Barbarigo
to Domenico Tron as *podestà* of Este (1490).

I ANOTHER NEW ROME?

'The Venetians are called new Romans.' This conceit, which the distinguished patrician, Bernardo Bembo (1433–1519), entered in his private commonplace book along with other texts in praise of the Venetian republic, was widely expressed in the fifteenth and sixteenth centuries. Respectfully, Benedetto Accolti equated Venice with Rome in a dialogue praising men of his time (c. 1460); jealously, another Florentine, who was ambassador to pope Pius II, complained in 1463: 'It is their constant boast that they are the successors of the Romans, and that the sovereignty of the world belongs to them.' The substance of the comparison lay in the political and economic power of Venice and the stable continuity of its institutions; by the end of the fifteenth century, the inheritance of Rome reborn in Venice had become a favourite theme for patriotic orations, literary dedications, historiography, art, popular verse and much else. Philippe de Commines, French ambassador in 1494–95, was one of many foreigners struck by the analogy, and wrote part of his description of Venice and the Venetians with it in mind. 'It is not to be expected that they should attain to the perfection and grandeur of the old Romans', he remarked, but added, 'they are in a fair way to be a very powerful people hereafter.'

It was common enough in this period for an Italian city's publicists to claim that it represented the rebirth of Roman civilization, as though this were the eternal standard of excellence; Leonardo Bruni had done it for Florence, emphasizing the city's foundation by republican Rome; Pier Candido Decembrio wrote of despotic Milan as the new Rome. But it was less common for outsiders with nothing to gain to join in such tributes; and also uncommon for a city which had no

Roman origins to be acclaimed in this way. The latter defect about the history of Venice was not, however, fully admitted, for its medieval chronicles had handed down a number of legends which attempted to repair the gap. The 'Veneti', it was claimed, were originally an Asiatic people, and the foundation of Padua and a Venetian kingdom by Antenor of Troy formed a parallel with Aeneas' foundation of Rome. The Florentine ambassador already quoted had expanded on this, according to Pius II: 'They say the successors of Trojan Aeneas ruled in their time, but now the sovereignty belongs to the descendants of Antenor.' According to another legend, patricians of the mainland, fleeing from barbaric invaders, were supposed to have established themselves in the lagoon on 25 March 421. Although this was much earlier than the invasions of Huns and Lombards, which may well have caused a mass exodus to the lagoon, it was not long after Alaric's entrance into Rome and may have been meant to imply a providential replacement of the one city by the other. March 25 was the recognized anniversary of the Annunciation to the Virgin Mary, and astrological tables were devised to prove further what a very propitious date this was. In the fifteenth century a decree of foundation by the consuls of Padua was invented: this was after the fire in Padua of 1420, which conveniently explained why the original document did not survive.

Because their city's rise to independence and prosperity had been so long and sustained, the Venetians had ample reason to congratulate themselves without needing a faked ancient history. They had been less troubled than most other Italians by German Emperors, the papacy with its temporal claims, foreign kings of Sicily, armed companies or parvenu military captains; they never submitted to a tyrant ruler. But even before such emphasis came to be placed on Rome, their patriotic dignity had been fostered by myths of antiquity and destiny. Above all, the cult of St Mark had enabled them to link their past with early Christianity, and to attribute their material success to his protecting favour.

5 Gentile Bellini's painting of a procession in the Piazza San Marco (1496), showing the completed basilica. Devout ceremony permeated Venetian political life in the heyday of the Imperial Age ▶

Tradition laid down that St Mark's remains had been stolen by two Venetian sailors in Moslem Alexandria and brought to Rialto in the year 829. The presence of the Evangelist gave Venice a sanctity little less than that of Rome with St Peter; in the eleventh century St Peter Damiani declared that Venice, too, was an apostolic city: Rome was the mother of all cities, but Venice a dutiful daughter. St Mark's basilica, under construction in its present form during the eleventh century but still being embellished in the fifteenth, was the saint's shrine and at the same time the shrine of Venetian patriotism: it was not the bishop's cathedral but the palace church of the doge, chief magistrate of the Venetians and mystical standard-bearer of St Mark. The Evangelist's emblem, a winged lion, provided a formidable symbol of primacy, force and justice: higher in the animal hierarchy and without the pagan associations of the Roman wolf, a more sacred and also more imperious lion than the rampant *marzocco* of the Florentines. Legends arose about St Mark's residence in Aquileia: that he wrote his Gospel there and the original manuscript still remained was believed even by the painstaking historian Marin Sanudo (1466–1536). Not

6, 7, 8, 9 Lions of St Mark: four variations, from the thirteenth to the fifteenth

only St Mark but the Archangel Raphael and even Christ himself were supposed to have appeared in the region of the lagoon; such visitors could only mean a high and holy destiny for Venice. 'Pax', the angelic injunction to St Mark when he landed at Rialto, was inscribed upon images of the winged lion holding the Gospel; Venetian chroniclers and publicists were not slow to interpret Venetian policy as peace-loving Christian service to the world, successfully performed through the favour and intercession of St Mark.

Two of the most censorious of medieval popes, Gregory VII and Innocent III, did not concur with this at all: Gregory in 1076 denied the doge his assumed authority in Dalmatia, and Innocent was to excommunicate the Venetians for diverting the Fourth Crusade there in 1202. It did not seem to matter. The peace made at Venice in 1177 between the heads of the world, pope Alexander III and the Emperor Frederick Barbarossa, went down in Venetian history as a memorable example of how the doge exerted a sort of third force of magistracy in Christendom; the outcome of the Fourth Crusade, after its diversion to Constantinople, became the Christian epic of Venice.

centuries, of the most common religious and political symbol of Venice.

Constantinople, the original 'new Rome', for long inspired the Venetians in their search for ancient identity and grandeur. Since the lagoon settlement had been part of the Byzantine empire for several centuries, there was a genuine though very late link with ancient civilization here. The eastern capital continued to be the city which Venice copied: St Mark's basilica was, for instance, modelled upon the church of the Holy Apostles in Constantinople. But the Crusaders' conquest in 1204 made the doge, if not emperor (this office fell to the count of Flanders), 'dominator of a quarter and half of a quarter of the empire of Rome' and gave the Venetians special cause to pose as the new (Byzantine) Romans. Largely responsible for evicting the Greek rulers of the empire, they saw themselves as its Catholic restorers and the true heirs of Constantine. In 1222 a proposal was even made to move the seat of Venetian government to Constantinople. Though this was rejected, there was at least a style of 'new Ravenna' if not of 'new Rome' about this period of Venetian history, until the fall of the Latin empire

10 Doge Jacopo Tiepolo (1229–49), who was responsible for having Venetian law codified, depicted in a thirteenth-century book of statutes.

11, 12 The bringing of St Mark's body to Venice was illustrated in mosaics (of the thirteenth century) on the front of the basilica. All four scenes, of which two are shown here, were intact when Gentile Bellini painted it in 1496; only one now survives.

in 1261; it evoked the last great age of eastern and western unity, the sixth-century empire of Justinian. The laws were codified and published by doge Tiepolo in 1229; Byzantine styles of the sixth century appear to have been imitated with deliberately archaic allusion in mosaic and relief sculpture at St Mark's, and upon the colonnaded façades of patrician houses. An absurdly unhistorical story was invented that Narses, Justinian's general, had retired as a monk to Venice, befriended the doge and built a church for him.

The period between 1261 and 1380 can be interpreted as an interval between this Byzantine imperial phase and the more Roman-inspired imperial age of Venice which followed. Such an interpretation may defy the economic evidence of increasing wealth and population in the later thirteenth and early fourteenth centuries which Venice like many other cities experienced; the Venetians had not lost their maritime possessions, and not even their trade in and beyond Constantinople was interrupted for long after 1261; their vigorous business enterprise is illustrated by the expedition into central Asia that same year by Marco Polo's father and uncle. Nevertheless, there are strong grounds for arguing that there was a hiatus, which lends definition to the period with which this book is specially concerned.

The prestige of Venice as a leading Christian power was seriously damaged by Michael Paleologos's recovery of Constantinople with Genoese aid. The chronicler Martino da Canale recognized this and exhorted the Venetians of his day to show themselves as worthy successors of doge Enrico Dandolo and repeat the achievements of 1204. Significantly, in 1277 the doge's title was modified to 'lord of lands and islands subject to the dogedom'. Plans to co-operate with king Charles I of Anjou, who ruled southern Italy from Naples, and resurrect the Latin empire of Constantinople were forestalled by the Sicilian rebellion of 1282, and further schemes up to 1320 came to nothing. But such failure (although it caused an acute financial crisis in 1282) and the revival of a small and precarious Greek empire were less serious than the expansion of rival interests in the eastern Mediterranean during this period, and the hostile designs of other western powers upon lands, ports and islands in the regions which Venice had dominated.

The Genoese were the principal enemies in overseas commerce. In the course of four maritime wars with Genoa, the Venetians were heavily defeated in 1298 at Curzola, one of their Dalmatian islands, and in 1353 off the island of Sapienza near their bases in southern Greece; in 1379 the Genoese even entered the Adriatic, won a victory at Zara and captured the city of Chioggia, within sight of Venice itself. Though there had also been Venetian victories, the expense and recurrence of these wars show how far Venice was from mastery of the seas. The armed convoys of state and privately owned galleys which the Venetians organized from the late thirteenth century onwards may illustrate the technical progress of navigation, great commercial enterprise and administrative skill, but they also reflect insecurity and the need to be on the defensive against Genoese, Catalan and other enemies or pirates.

Meanwhile, Venice had also to face hostility during the fourteenth century from the king of Hungary, who belonged to the Angevin royal family of Naples. His claims to Dalmatia led to war, and in 1358 Venice lost possession of Ragusa, which had been held almost uninterruptedly since the eleventh century; his allies in the hinterland of Venice, particularly Francesco da Carrara of Padua, aided the Genoese in their crucial hostilities of 1379–80.

Moreover, the Venetian régime was more troubled internally during this period than perhaps at any time during its millennium of independence. In many ways Venice was quite unlike the other leading Italian cities in its governing institutions. Not only did the magistracy of the doge survive, even if restricted in power, but the patriciate was almost wholly mercantile; proprietorship of lands or private jurisdiction carried no weight in the government of the commune and the many guilds were relatively humble bodies of craftsmen and artisans: they never represented predominant economic interests or attempted to dominate communal institutions. The contrast with Florence is striking. Nevertheless, there were some parallels with other Italian cities in the tensions which occurred in the later thirteenth century, and few others apart from Florence found an effective solution. Many merchants whose fortunes and status had risen during the boom of the last two centuries feared that either older established patrician families or newcomers and more recent careerists might try to seize control of the greater council of the commune (*maggior consiglio*). They suspected that a doge of long-standing family dignity, Lorenzo Tiepolo (1268–75), had planned to construct a despotism upon hyper-aristocratic and popular support, and were alarmed in 1289 by the attempted election of his son Jacopo, who might have followed this example. A series of measures between 1297 and 1323 prevented recurrence of this danger by regulating membership of the greater council and so of access to any higher council or office – regulations which had the subtle effect of vastly increasing the membership, swamping the more ancient families, and creating a body of registered patricians whose descendants were jealous to retain their privilege and generally prepared to conform to the dominant interests.

This system of enclosed, if broadly enclosed, government, was not established without opposition. The most violent resistance was led by Baiamonte Tiepolo in 1310, and his defeat illustrates the practical difficulty of either organizing an attack from outside or co-ordinating rebellion in a waterbound maze of a city, without gates, walls, escape routes or central rallying-points. Two fourteenth-century doges protested in their own ways against a system which limited their scope for effective leadership. From the brilliant young Andrea Dandolo (doge from 1343 to 1354) came a moral protest, expressed in the historical writings in which he evoked the name of his heroic ancestor of the Fourth Crusade, and deplored a decline of Venetian virtue, unity and faith. From his elderly successor, Marin Falier (doge 1354–56), one of those who had been most determined to bring Baiamonte Tiepolo to trial and was obsessed with fear of aristocratic conspiracy, came an active protest, invoking the labour force of the Arsenal against his patrician enemies, for which he was executed.

Mid fourteenth-century Venice impressed Petrarch as 'strong in power but stronger in virtue; built on solid marble but more stably and solidly established on the more secure foundations of the citizens' concord'. Petrarch was a well-entertained visitor, and his encomium disregards the internal political struggles, the visitations of plague, and the challenge overseas (including in 1363–64 a settlers' revolt in Crete, the most valuable colony), all of which disturbed the republic's serenity. On the other hand, he did much to nurture the nostalgia about ancient Rome, which was to grow in the following century. His friend, doge Andrea Dandolo, who suggested in his historical writings that the office he held demanded all the finest qualities of the Roman emperors from Claudius to Justinian, was exhorted by him to practise imperial statesmanship in the interests of all Italy. 'Your nation . . . traces back its fame to the most remote antiquity', he wrote to Dandolo in 1351, in an attempt to persuade him to seek peace with Genoa for the sake of Italy. 'Would that instead you could fight against Persians, Arabs, Thracians, or Illyrians . . . by the arts of peace India, Britain, and Ethiopia would be made to fear you.' Three years later Petrarch wrote to the harassed Dandolo, 'Be another Trajan!' In all this he was disappointed.

13 Doges of the Dandolo family illustrated in a sixteenth-century descriptive list of patrician families; patricians tended to identify Venetian history with their ancestors.

Petrarch did not live long enough to see the inspiring war effort of 1379–80 under doge Andrea Contarini: Vettor Pisani's naval blockade of the Genoese in Chioggia was relieved at last by the arrival of Carlo Zeno's fleet, and the enemy surrendered in June 1380. Probably Petrarch would have said that the events of this final Punic War of the Venetians vindicated all his hyperbole about their virtue, but whether or not they created or vindicated Venetian morale, they seem to coincide with the beginning of a new period in Venetian history. Over the next 200 years much continued as before, and there were many new times of trouble, but the régime was enhanced, and its stability more assured. For the last time until the seventeenth century the greater council was opened to an appreciable number of new members: as many as thirty were co-opted as a reward for their contributions to the war effort. Economic recovery was slow at first, but sure before the end of the century, and with the rapid expansion of both mainland and overseas dominion, which will be discussed in later chapters, it is not surprising that Venice came to be acclaimed as a new (western) Rome. For this is perhaps the most distinctive trait of the second imperial age: the cult of St Mark and the associations with the east remained, and after 1453, when Constantinople fell to the Turks, there was special reason to acclaim Venice as the new 'new Rome'. But Venetian foreign policy, political rhetoric, learning and art all became more closely involved with the rest of Italy, and acquired many tones of the revival of antiquity in vogue there.

The astonishing increase of Venetian territory and opulence in the first two decades of the fifteenth century prompted doge Tommaso Mocenigo to boast, in a famous speech to the senators in 1423, that if this continued Venice would control the wealth of Christendom ('sarete padroni dell'oro e della Cristianità'). Most of the panegyrics, however, came from outside. Greeks wrote no less enthusiastically than westerners about Venice, inadequate though Venetian help had been to save Constantinople in 1453. Cardinal Bessarion, in a letter to the doge in 1469, described Venice as almost another Constantinople: indisputably it had now become the leading Christian city of the Mediterranean. Pope Pius II (1458–64), bitter though he was about some aspects of Venetian policy, contradicted himself at one point in his memoirs, or *Commentaries*, by conceding that, 'today the Venetians are the most powerful people on both land and sea and seem not unfitted for the larger empire to which they aspire.'

Humanist scholars were naturally fascinated by the spectacle of Venetian power. Although he had written a defence of despotism on behalf of the Carrara lords of Padua, Pier Paolo Vergerio early in the fifteenth century expressed surprise that the Venetian nation, so like that of the Romans, had no historian of its empire. The rebuke was not answered for some time, though there were distinguished aspirants to the task. These included Lorenzo Valla, philologist and philosopher; the historian Biondo of Forlì, who had even made a start with a treatise on *The Origin and Deeds of the Venetians* which he dedicated to doge Foscari in 1454; and Poggio Bracciolini, Florentine wit, Latinist and papal secretary. Though Poggio in his essay *On Nobility* (c. 1440) had derided the Venetian patricians as traders who, however dull or stupid, were esteemed as noble above the wisest of citizens excluded from their rank, in about 1450 he wrote a treatise *In Praise of the Venetian Republic*, describing it as the perfect fusion of aristocracy and monarchy imagined by Aristotle.

A pedantic scholar who had been teaching rhetoric at Udine eventually became the first official historian of Venice, under the grandiose pen-name of Marcus Antonius Sabellicus (1453–1506). The outcome, written at speed between 1484 and 1486 for monthly payment, was a hack's work, which reproduced all the old legends in a ponderous imitation of classical Latin. But Sabellicus's thesis that Venice was even superior to ancient Rome was one which went down well with the Venetian patriciate. Marin Sanudo revealed the vanity of his caste in following Sabellicus. In the preface to his *Lives of the Doges* (*c.* 1520), for instance, he declared that even in its origins Venice was superior: not founded by shepherds (he presumably meant Romulus and Remus) but by the powerful and nobly born. In his preface to the *De Bello Gallico* (1495), the evocative title he and several other historians gave to their accounts of the Italian invasion of king Charles VIII of France, he even hailed doge Agostino Barbarigo (1486–1501) as 'the new Augustus'. 'More arduous and important matters have happened under your dogeship than under any other prince,' he assured Barbarigo in his dedication, and acclaimed him for saving the peace of Italy. Terms of praise for doge Barbarigo were no less pompous at the more popular levels of literature: 'Prince of my new Rome', the poet Ventura di Malgate addressed him, worthy of comparison with Numa Pompilius, Cato the Censor, Scipio, Fabius and other ancient worthies both mythical and historical: 'A Ulysses in astuteness, a new Brutus in justice, a new Camillus in gaining victory, lover of universal well-being.'

Rhetoric, spoken and written, was far from being the only way in which these pretensions were expressed. In the later fifteenth century the tombs of the doges, enormous sculptural structures set against the walls of Venetian churches, were devised in the form of triumphal arches and embellished with figures of Roman soldiers and battle trophies; in the 1480s the new decorations to the doge's palace included a medley of bas-reliefs of shields, helmets and other evocative paraphernalia, with pompous and puzzling devices in Roman lettering. SPQV is straightforward, but OCFA–LFET has been ingeniously read as *Omnes Contigit Felicibus Armis – Latos Fines Extremae Terrae*, which might be translated, 'with all-conquering arms, she [Venice] touched upon all the wide bounds of the furthermost earth'. The conceit of being neo-Roman inspired some Venetian patricians to claim their direct descent from Roman families because of similar sounding names. The Cornaro family called themselves 'Cornelii' and ordered paintings to illustrate the triumphs of their supposed ancestor, Publius Cornelius Scipio; the Marcelli and the Emiliani were also believed to be Roman

14, 15 The earliest pseudo-antique medal in Venice: an imitation Roman sesterce of the emperor Galba, designed in 1393 by Marco Sesto, who worked in the Mint. The reverse shows a female personification of Venice.

16, 17, 18 Above left, opening page of Niccolò da Correggio's pastoral drama *Cephalo e l'Aurora*, copied (1497) for a Venetian patrician: the device 'SPQV' appears here suggestively. Above, the tomb as a heroic monument: Jacopo Marcello (d. 1484) was killed in action against the Turks at Gallipoli. Left, trophies of war and lions: details from decorative sculpture of the late fifteenth century in the doge's palace.

families; the Barbo family claimed descent from the Roman Ehenobarbus, founder of Parma. Others, less fortunately named, such as the Moro or Barbaro families, could not compete, but had the comfort of jocose assurances that they were neither Moors nor barbarians. The epitaph of the young Ermolao Barbaro, the scholarly paragon who died at Rome in 1493, preserves both the stale pun and the coupling of the two cities to Venice's greater credit: 'Ermolao Barbaro, who rejected every barbarity . . . the city of Venice gave him life; Renowned Rome gave him death.'

There were many absurdities about this patrician cult of antiquity. Did the Venetian patricians see themselves as Romans of the republic and of the empire simultaneously? Could the doge reasonably be called Augustus rather than first consul? How could the comparison fit when the Venetians depended so much more on naval than military power? Philippe de Commines had emphasized their inferiority to Rome on this point, and declared, 'Their bodies are not so able to bear the fatigues of war, neither are they of such a martial genius.' Perhaps this was unfair; if commanders serving Venice on land were usually hired mercenaries, patricians commissioned as *provveditori* were in charge of operations; there were local militia levies and the *stradiotti* or light cavalry recruited from Greeks and Albanians. But there was no regular system of Venetian legions, and little danger of military rebellion as in ancient Rome, beyond the treachery of an individual mercenary, such as Carmagnola, who was executed in 1432. The cult of antiquity, however, found expression in naval terms as well. 'The Venetians are the soldiers of the sea,' was one of Bernardo Bembo's entries in his commonplace book; the new gateway to the Arsenal was in 1460 one of the first examples in Venice of the applied forms of Roman architecture. Vettor Fausto, the distinguished professor of Greek in Padua, even designed a neo-Roman quinquireme, which was launched in 1529, though found to be impractical.

Vain though much of this may seem, the idea of Venice as a new Rome, even an improvement on Rome, continued to gain

19 The land gateway of the Arsenal (1460); the terrace of statuary in front is of the late seventeenth century.

subscribers. The fascination it held, whether from respect or envy, among articulate Florentines, has already been illustrated; it is ironical that citizens of the rival republic did so much to inflate the reputation of Venice. Resentment and derision flourished also: Poggio's earlier reflections and the ambassadorial comments to Pius II have already been mentioned. In 1470 a Florentine merchant, Benedetto Dei, wrote a peculiar open letter to the government of Venice, declaring that not only was Florence the older and more truly Roman city, but that Venetians, apart from Paduan descendants of 'Antenor's traitorous breed', were a mixed stock of Slavs and fishermen; Niccolò Machiavelli, like Poggio, considered that Venetian 'nobility' was ignoble, and his political writings do not suggest that he was markedly impressed by the Venetian constitution and empire.

But it was much more fashionable to eulogize Venice. The precedent set by Petrarch, enhanced during the period of political alliance with Venice after 1425, and by humanist contacts between the two cities, had reached a climax by the end of the fifteenth century. Domination of their city by the Medici had previously led disaffected Florentines into congenial exile in Venice, and after the Medici fell in 1494, Venice was

29

acclaimed by many Florentine aristocrats as a model for their reconstituted republic. A great council which controlled offices by election, a smaller council or senate, even a life magistrate (1502), were among their new experiments, although there was no similar confinement of politics to a patrician caste. The restoration of the Medici in 1512, and the failure of the free republic of 1527–29, made Florentine tributes all the more flattering. The patrician historian Francesco Guicciardini declared that Venice had 'the best government of any city not only in our own times but also in the classical world'; Donato Giannotti reflected in his famous *Dialogue on the Republic of the Venetians* (written in 1525–26, published in 1543) on the excellence of Venetian institutions, in contrast to the unstable ones of Florence, and the remarkable survival of Venice amidst the disasters of Italy.

Venetian writers did their part, too, in praising their own state and society, none more than Gasparo Contarini in his book *On the Venetian Magistrates* (written in 1524, published in 1540); but Florentine eloquence had done most to create and sustain the tradition. That scurrilous Tuscan, Pietro Aretino, made his own contribution to the theme of Venetian superiority in a letter of 1530 to doge Andrea Gritti, thanking him for the refuge he had enjoyed in Venice after the final collapse of the Florentine republic and the devastation and occupation of Italy by French and Imperial arms. 'O universal fatherland!' he wrote, 'O common liberty! How much greater would the woes of Italy have been if your goodness had been less! Here is the refuge of her nations, here the security of her riches, and here her honour is saved.' A citizen of Rome itself, the wistful civic patriot Marcello Alberini, made a similar if less eloquent acknowledgment in his chronicle of the Imperial armies' Sack of Rome in 1527: 'only Venice now upholds the honour of Italy'. Paradoxically, though they had failed their allies in the defence of both eastern and western Rome in 1453 and 1527, the Venetians' own reputation as new Romans seems to have been increased by these disasters.

20 The greater council in session: an engraving of 1566. Voting is in progress; linen ballots placed in a red urn were 'ayes', in a green urn 'noes'

ORDINE DEL PRESENTE CONSEGLIO DI VINETIA

A Il principe e tuoi Consoltieri   E Vn caio di x. et uno Auog.or   M Fratelli et fioli di Principe Q Esltero cauo diex   sano le balotte.
bondi, et da una a cari si 40. F Vno Censore.   N Cauaglieri.   R Li Sig.ri sopra le pompe.   X Li s6 balottini
et da laltra sin solo.   G Auditori noui.   O Dottori.   S Banca delli uecchi.   V capelli doue li balottini por-
B C Secretarij che balotte. I Vno auogador di comun.   P Sedia doue il gran Can- T Doue senta il Canceli. tano à uotare le balotte.
D Il Cancelier grande quado sta K Vn cauo, de x.   celiero strida quelloshi ha, et grande.   Z Auditori uecchi.

TRADE AND DOMINION OVERSEAS

The Venetian empire was essentially a commercial enterprise: this fact underlies all the would-be Roman pomp and ceremony, the *pax veneta*, rule of law and incidental benefits the lordship of St Mark was supposed to bring. The most vital organs of the empire were, therefore, warehouses, ships' holds, barges and pack-horses; its administrators were consuls, customs officers, merchants' factors and notaries; it greatly exceeded the range of dominion overseas (*stato da mar*) and overland (*terraferma*), with which these chapters are mainly concerned. In essence it comprised the total field of investment and interest of Venetians, particularly patricians, over a great sweep of the known world, from Bruges and London to Trebizond, Aleppo, Alexandria and beyond.

Though St Mark was celestial patron of the empire, by the sixteenth century the ancient gods were also involved in its iconography. Mercury and Neptune, the gods of commerce and the sea, appear as the patrons of Venice upon the enormous view of the city engraved in 1500, probably by Jacopo de' Barbari, for the German merchant Anton Kolb; and they were carved on a gigantic scale by Jacopo Sansovino, to be placed above the stairs in the courtyard of the doge's palace in 1566. Mars also appeared as the companion of Neptune. The pair of them appear on the monument to the naval commander Benedetto Pesaro (d. 1503) in the church of the Frari, and with a tame-looking lion between them on one of Veronese's ceiling paintings for the *sala del collegio* in the doge's palace (1575–77). Veronese's disregard for St Mark in his allegories was even more daring in a scene he had painted for the hall of the council of ten (1553–54) in which Juno, not the Evangelist, is shown dropping

33

◄ 21 Mars and Neptune with the campanile and lion of St Mark between them: Veronese's painting in the *sala del collegio* (1575–77).

22 Mercury and Neptune at the head of the courtyard staircase in the doge's palace, where the doge stood at solemn receptions.

gifts upon Venice, a buxom female whose back rests against a globe and whose free hand rests lightly on the head of a half-obscured lion.

Juno's gifts are not only the emblems of political power and peace, but also a shower of gold coins. This was well conceived, for the gold ducat was an even more widely distributed symbol of Venetian ascendancy than the winged lion. First struck in 1284, by 1423, according to doge Mocenigo, ducats were being minted at the rate of a million every year. They hardly ever varied in gold content and design, and during the fifteenth century displaced all other coins as the standard of monetary soundness and stability. Even the Florentines and the papacy came to prefer the word 'ducat' to 'florin' for their own gold coins; the Venetian exemplar was imitated from east to west, by the Mamluk sultans of Cairo, by Mehmed the Conqueror at Constantinople, and by Ferdinand and Isabella of Spain.

23, 24 Mercury and Neptune: detail from the de' Barbari map of Venice (1500).

35

25 Tomb of Benedetto Pesaro (d. 1503). The relief carvings below refer to his victories against the Turks in the Ionian islands: left, Leucas; right, Cephalonia.

26, 27 Gold ducat of Agostino Barbarigo's dogeship. Obverse, St Mark presents his standard to the doge; reverse, Christ in a nimbus.

This sound gold and silver coinage symbolized the collective wealth which, by the time of doge Mocenigo's speech in 1423, seemed to exceed that of any other commercial power in Christendom. It was not a wealth based upon money, unlike that of many Tuscan and Genoese merchants who provided international credit and exchange facilities, nor to any great extent upon industrial production, although there were in Venice tanners, silk-weavers, glass-blowers and many other craftsmen working on a limited scale; its basis remained the widely diversified import-export business and freight carrying (which included the transport of humans as slaves and pilgrims) already mentioned.

Moreover, the régime of the Venetian patricians rested upon their own retention of the main opportunities for capital investment in long-distance trade, its supervision and protection. No other state in the fourteenth and fifteenth centuries reserved for its hereditary governors such commercial privileges, or maintained such extensive powers of economic administration. Not only were there bond warehouses, customs offices and judicial tribunals by means of which the patricians supervised and taxed every species of goods in transit from land and sea through the compulsory emporium of Venice, but the Arsenal, probably the biggest industrial complex of medieval Europe, had prescriptive rights for the employment of skilled labour, and included the state shipbuilding yard, dry and wet docks, rope and sail factories, and, by the late fifteenth century, gunpowder

28 The Arsenal in 1500. In the foreground freight-carrying round ships or cogs are seen at anchor.

mills and an ordnance depot. State-owned galleys, the management of which was auctioned to an individual patrician before each voyage, provided an unrivalled, safe, regular and rapid transport for non-bulky freight, travelling down the Adriatic and then east to Alexandria, Syria and Constantinople, or west

37

into the Atlantic to Flanders and England. But there was also a vast amount of shipping in private ownership. Doge Mocenigo's figures estimate a total of 45 galleys, state and private, and 300 cargo ships of over 100 tons capacity, with hundreds of smaller craft working in the Adriatic. Only the Genoese, who did not use galleys except for fighting, but who in 1424 had 63 ships of high capacity for the heavy cargoes in which they specialized, could show anything approaching this enormous merchant marine fleet.

As a great commercial organism, the Venetian empire remained strong in its readiness to adapt to changed opportunities. As well as its constant use of the German and Italian hinterland and the Adriatic, its opportunist development in the eastern Mediterranean has already been mentioned, whether pro-Byzantine, pro-Moslem, pro-Crusader, or anti-Byzantine; likewise its use from the early fourteenth century of the Atlantic in place of the overland route to the north, where Mediterranean goods could be traded for Flemish cloth and English wool. Interest in the western Mediterranean increased noticeably in the later fifteenth century and was another symptom of this resilient enterprise. State galleys were routed to Aigues Mortes, the Catalan coast and North Africa, and new markets were developed in these regions; cloth from England or 'spices' from Syria and Alexandria might, for instance, be sold there, and goods such as leather, honey and wax acquired; but such was the diversity of trade that it is difficult to trace any exact pattern in the exchange of commodities. The western trend reflected an acceptance of declining trade in the Black Sea region, a trend which began long before the Turks gained control of the Straits.

Similarly, the challenge of Portuguese competition in the 'spice' trade after Vasco da Gama's voyage in 1497, did not harm Venetian business so seriously and irrevocably as used to be thought. Admittedly there was apprehension: in 1502 a special advisory board on the spice trade was set up 'to provide remedies lest the king of Portugal takes the silver and gold out of our hands, to the manifest ruin of our business affairs and

29 Reception of the ambassador Domenico Trevisan at Cairo, 1512; Venice had long-standing relations with the Mamluk rulers of Egypt through the spice trade.

posterity'. The building of a Suez Canal was discussed, and Venetian ambassadors were instructed to convince the Mamluk sultan in Cairo of the need for active measures to repel the Portuguese from the Indian Ocean. Yet much of the alarm proved false. Pepper was the only spice over which the Portuguese offered serious competition; but their pepper was generally of inferior quality, and even if it became available at Antwerp as well as Lisbon, this market was no more convenient than Venice for many middlemen of the growing European consumer market. Nor was Portuguese pepper drastically cheaper since the costs of transport, which included naval warfare in the Indian Ocean, caused the crown to place a tax upon it. The spice trade in Venice went through a bad period from about 1496 to 1520, when supplies were short and prices high; but there is much else to explain this besides Portuguese competition. The Venetian-Turkish war of 1499–1503, Turkish

39

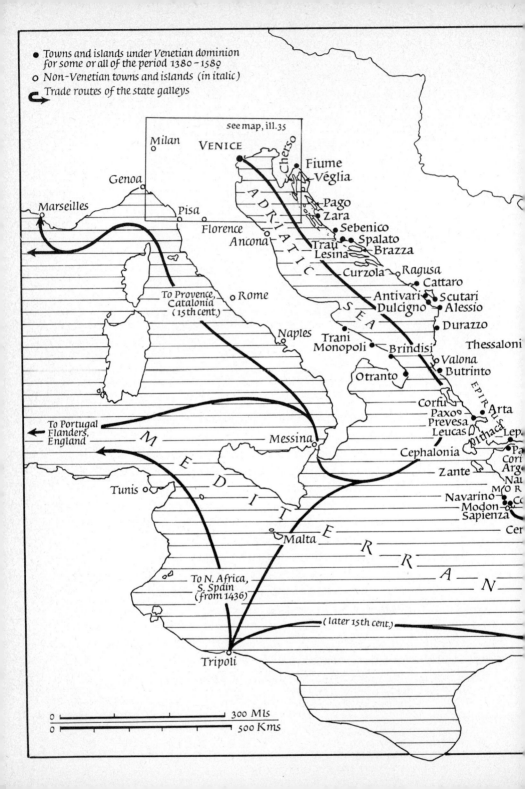

● Towns and islands under Venetian dominion
   for some or all of the period 1380–1589
○ Non-Venetian towns and islands (in italic)
↪ Trade routes of the state galleys

Milan

see map, ill.35

VENICE

Genoa

Cherso

Fiume
Véglia

Marseilles

Pisa

Pago
Zara

Florence
Ancona

Sebenico
Spalato
Trau
Lesina
Brazza

To Provence,
Catalonia
(15th cent.)

Rome

A D R I A T I C

Curzola *Ragusa*
Cattaro
Antivari Scutari
Dulcigno Alessio

S E A

Durazzo

Thessaloni

Naples

Trani
Monopoli
Brindisi
Valona
Butrinto

Otranto

E P I R U S

To Portugal
Flanders,
England

M

Messina

Corfu
Paxo Arta
Prevesa
Leucas *Ithaca* *Lep*
Cephalonia *Pa*
Cori
Zante *Arg*
Nau
Navarino *Co*
Modon M O R
Sapienza
Cer

Tunis

E

D

I

T

Malta

E

R

R

A

N

To N. Africa,
S. Spain
(from 1436)

(later 15th cent.)

Tripoli

0 _____ 300 Mls
0 _____ 500 Kms

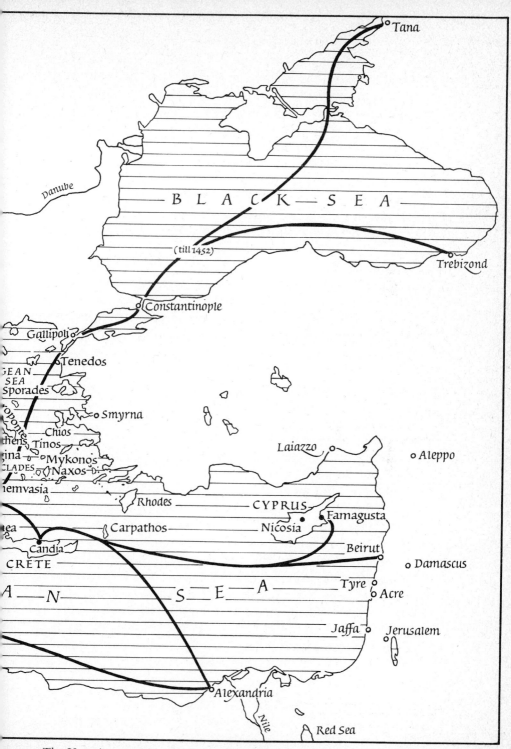

Danube

B L A C K — S E A

Tana

Trebizond

(till 1452)

Constantinople

Gallipoli

Tenedos

GEAN
SEA
Sporades

opone

Smyrna

Chios

thens

Tinos

gina

Mykonos

CLADES

Naxos

iemvasia

Rhodes

CYPRUS

Laiazzo

Aleppo

Famagusta

Nicosia

ea

Carpathos

Beirut

Candia

CRETE

Damascus

A

N

S

E

A

Tyre

Acre

Jaffa

Jerusalem

Alexandria

Nile

Red Sea

30 The Venetian maritime empire, 1380–1580.

wars in Persia disturbing the overland spice routes, war in northern Italy, and instability in Egypt until the Ottomans conquered the Mamluks in 1517 and restored normal business conditions, were all to blame.

Whatever remains to be said about Turks and Portuguese, historians have proved that more pepper and cotton were being re-exported from Venice in the 1560s than when doge Mocenigo quoted statistics to the senators in 1423. Though the state galley system was obsolete by the middle decades of the sixteenth century, and competition in the carrying trade had been increasing since the later fifteenth century, there was a boom in the building of larger ships, and an increase in home-manufactured exports, including woollen textiles, an industry which had grown up from almost nothing since 1520. The Venetian trade empire was still flexible and flourishing.

Empire, however, is better understood as dominion and administration, and for Venice the flag followed trade to a greater extent than it did for any other Mediterranean city. This process had begun in the Adriatic; security for the trade in timber, salt, corn and wine, and the need for Venetian ships to take shelter along the sea's protective eastern shore, fretted with safe anchorages and islands, had led to preferential treaties or subjection being imposed on the Slav-inhabited ports. From the beginning of the eleventh century, the doge had taken the style of 'duke of Dalmatia', and Venice, the *Dominante*, was by papal concession in 1177 mystically married to the sea within the 'Venetian gulf', as the Adriatic north of Corfu was possessively called. Trade within the Byzantine empire, Fatimid Egypt and the Latin kingdom of Jerusalem, brought privileged enclaves in many ports for Venetian merchants, and dominion in the east came after the great distribution of Byzantine spoils in 1204. Yet in their first imperial age the Venetians' concern was only for the positions most useful to their commerce: particularly Modon and Coron, on the south-west tip of the Greek mainland, and Crete, perfectly sited bases and junctions on their routes of maritime trade. Their settled dominions

31 Modon, the important Venetian naval station on the southern tip of Greece, lost to the Turks in 1501.

overseas in the thirteenth century consisted mainly of Crete and parts of Negroponte (Euboea), where they had only a limited jurisdiction. The Cyclades were seized independently by Venetian patricians to be held as fiefs of the Latin empire, not of Venice, and Venetian claims upon the Greek mainland, to much of Morea and Epirus, and to the Ionian islands including Corfu, were not pursued for long.

A new imperial age, or a second and greater imperial thrust of Venetian power overseas, can be detected in the period after 1380. The succession crisis of the Angevin dynasty of Naples and the collapse of its eastern pretensions, the weakness of the restored Byzantine empire, the shortage of heirs to fiefs on the Greek mainland and islands, and the growth of Ottoman power from the 1350s all added to the opportunities of Venice.

43

The Turks are too often regarded as the creeping mortality of the Venetian empire; in some respects they provided a stimulus, and gave Venetian dominion a protective appeal for local populations. There was no simple pattern in the way Venice acquired, held or lost new territory; but dominion, until the beginning of the sixteenth century, was on balance increasing.

The first wave of expansion came immediately after the Genoese war of 1379–80 (war of Chioggia), the immediate cause of which had been a quarrel over the Venetian right to garrison Tenedos, at the entrance to the Dardanelles. In the Aegean region, Negroponte passed almost wholly under Venetian jurisdiction in 1383; Argos and Nauplia were bought in 1388 from the widow of Pietro Cornaro; Mykonos and Tinos were inherited by the republic, apparently with the clamorous approval of their inhabitants, in 1390; even Athens was taken under Venetian protection from 1394 to 1402. At the southern end of the Adriatic, Corfu, Paxo and the neighbouring base of Butrinto on the mainland, were ceded by the island's notables in 1386, a devolution which was confirmed by payment to king Ladislas, the *de facto* heir to Angevin Naples, in 1402. To Butrinto were added Parga (1401), Prevesa (1499) and other mainland fortresses, so that a Venetian foothold in Epirus, one of the lost opportunities of the years after 1204, became a reality at last. Further up the coast in Albania, there were other Venetian acquisitions: Durazzo, Alessio, and the inland city of Scutari became Venetian in 1392; other cities followed, as far north as Cattaro (1420).

All round the coasts of Greece there were new Venetian occupations, some temporary, some long-lasting, in the fifteenth century, and the population of Venetian dominions was swollen with emigrants from Turkish-held territory. To secure the Gulf of Corinth, Lepanto was acquired in 1407 from its Albanian lord, possibly by purchase but more probably by force, and on the opposite coast the archbishop of Patras leased to Venice his important city for some years. Round to the northeast, Thessalonika voluntarily became Venetian in 1423, though it passed to the Turks seven years later; in 1451 the island of Aegina came to Venice by inheritance, and the northern Sporades were annexed in 1453; the duchy of Naxos or the Archipelago, formerly the fief of the Sanudo family, came under direct rule for some years after 1494. The mainland of southern Greece (Morea, or the Peloponnese) was more seriously coveted by Venice in the fifteenth century than at any time since 1204. Navarino (Zonchio) was added in 1417 to the territory of Modon and Coron, and in the 1420s a negotiated annexation of nearly all Morea was being considered. This again seemed a possibility in the early stages of the Turkish war which broke out in 1463, considered by pope Pius II himself as an imperialist war of aggression until he reconciled it with his larger plans for a crusade. The Venetians, he wrote in his memoirs,

thought the time had come when they could subjugate the largest and most famous peninsula of Greece. . . . They were well aware of the profits to be derived from the Peloponnese . . . that it is a region most convenient for the whole world's trade, a veritable abode of merchants, abounding in wine, wheat and everything requisite for human existence. They were possessed with the desire of conquering a very rich province. . . . This course was urged upon them by an overcrowded city which could no longer endure itself. Those they call nobles, who have control of the government, had increased to a remarkable degree, though all are slaves to the sordid occupations of trade. They thought they ought to send out a colony and that there was no better place to found one than the Peloponnese.

The first triumphs of the war in mainland Greece did not last long, and the feat of reconstructing the Hexamilion, or defensive wall across the Isthmus of Corinth, was not sufficient to hold back the Turks; but at least Venice gained and kept Monemvasia.

The most important new possessions, however, were acquired in the least lawful ways, and not simply out of reaction to Turkish power, but also for fear of the new Aragonese kingdom of Naples, which had revived Angevin ambitions and intrigues in the east. Both the Tocco dynasty of the populous Ionian islands and the Lusignan dynasty of Cyprus were dispossessed with a suave ruthlessness. Zante was seized in 1482, and the other Ionian islands which the Turks occupied shortly after this were captured by the Venetians in the war of 1499–1503; Cephalonia and Ithaca were retained, and only Santa Maura (Leucas) handed back to the Turks in the peace treaty. In Cyprus, although James III (d. 1473) had usurped the throne from his sister, the survival of his Venetian widow Caterina Cornaro, and the death of their only child, gave the republic a pretext to take over the island quietly. Caterina Cornaro was virtually imprisoned by the Venetian forces in occupation, and by 1489 had been persuaded to abdicate and make a total transference of the island to Venice.

It would be nonsense to stretch too far the paradox that the Ottomans were a benefit to Venice; enormous expense, devastation and losses were incurred because of them. Nevertheless, their main objectives, from the time they first became formidable as overland raiders in the fourteenth century, were tribute in the form of slaves and money and the freedom to hire western mercenary contingents and craftsmen, rather than the dislocation of Venetian commerce or the seizure of harbours and islands. Venetians did not greatly mind the weakening of the Byzantine empire, and rejoiced in any setbacks to the Genoese; Serbian and Bulgarian losses on the European mainland concerned them little. Religion was a secondary issue; the Venetians had always traded with Moslems in Egypt and Syria as readily as with schismatic Greek Christians, and the Ottomans were not trying to convert by the sword.

The outlook for Venice became less attractive in the second decade of the fifteenth century. The Turks had advanced overland to strike the Adriatic coast of Albania, where they captured Valona in 1414. They were also developing naval power at their Aegean bases of Gallipoli (which they had held since 1357) and Smyrna (captured in 1402) with the skills of subjected Greeks and western shipbuilders. Pietro Loredan's victory at Gallipoli in 1416 proved Venetian superiority, but after the

32 Caterina Cornaro, ex-queen of Cyprus: a portrait identified in Gentile Bellini's painting of a miracle of the Holy Cross.

Turks had taken Thessalonika (1430), Constantinople (1453), and Piraeus (1455) a formidable number of excellent harbours lay in their control. They were now in a position to raid not only the Danube basin and the Balkans, but southern Greece and the islands, in fact the whole Venetian empire *da mar*. Quite apart from official warfare, Turkish freebooters became a growing danger in the Adriatic as well as in the seas round Greece. Fra Felix Fabri graphically described this peril in his account of a pilgrimage voyage in 1480, when the galley he was aboard narrowly missed the Turkish raiding fleet bound for Otranto. Two years later the Turks gained a new base for sea raiding, Castelnuovo at the entrance (*bocche*) to the deep fiord of Cattaro.

Nevertheless, even if the Turks were becoming a greater threat on the seas than 'Christian' piracy had been in the past, official hostilities were not inevitable. To pay tribute may have been humiliating, but it was not ruinous, and Turkish possession of major seaports did not curtail commerce except in time of war. Thessalonika was a flourishing centre for Venetian merchants after 1430, and galleys continued to go to Constantinople after 1453. While the Venetian posture as armed champion and even martyr of Christendom had its attractions as propaganda, and eloquent voices in Italy, Poggio and Guarino for instance, affected to believe in it, the true position was more opportunist. Christian rivalries were almost as worrying to the Venetians; the sacrifice of Thessalonika in 1430 left them free to plan an abortive campaign against Genoese Chios; in 1448 they sought Turkish help against the independent Albanian leader Skanderbeg; and Aragonese designs provoked their rapid eviction of the Tocchi and the Lusignans. Thus there was a certain justice in Pius II's diatribe on the subject of Venetian hard bargaining at the Congress of Mantua in 1459, when he was hoping to launch a crusade, though he did not take into account that the Venetians had bargained just as hard in 1201–02, nor that they had at least been more prompt than the papacy to send relief to Constantinople in 1453. 'Alas! Venetian race,' he wrote, 'how much of your ancient character have you lost! Too much intercourse with the Turks has made you the friend of the Mohammedans.'

'Friend' is perhaps an unfair word for the pope to have used; no other Christian power spent so heavily on defence and war against the Turks as did the Venetians. Nevertheless, the duration of war was only for a small fraction of the whole period: 1463–79, 1499–1503, 1537–40, 1570–73. Remarkably few of the main Venetian possessions were lost during the fifteenth century. Negroponte (1470) was the most serious. 'If Negroponte is lost, all the state of the Levant right up to Istria will be lost with it,' the panicky galley captain Girolamo Longo wrote in June 1470. 'Now it seemed that Venetian grandeur

33 Turkish raiders, 1575.

was abased and our pride extinguished,' wrote Domenico
Malipiero, describing the fearful scenes of lamentation when the
government at last admitted the disaster. All this was unduly
pessimistic. Close to the Turkish-occupied mainland, which its
anchorages face, Negroponte had obviously been vulnerable for
a long time; though agriculturally productive and in a strategic
position, its loss was more than compensated by the acquisitions
of Venice already mentioned. Argos was also lost, and Scutari,
after a heroic defence, was another major sacrifice in the peace
treaty of 1479, but the annual tribute – 10,000 ducats – was
nothing if set against Venetian profits and revenues from overseas trade and dominion; and it is doubtful whether it was paid
after 1481. Mehmed the Conqueror did not covet Venetian
commercial power as he coveted, in his dreams, Rome's prestige.

It was insulting bluff on the grand vizir's part when he told
the Venetian ambassador in 1499 that if in the past the doge of
Venice had married the sea, in future the sultan would be the
bridegroom. The ambassador was coldly polite in his explanation that this picturesque old ceremony, conceded by both

49

popes and emperors, was supposed only to refer to the gulf above Corfu. Although in the ensuing war the group of southern bases, Modon, Coron and Navarino, were lost with their dependent territory, and likewise Lepanto in the Gulf of Corinth, the Venetian empire in the sixteenth century extended almost unbrokenly down the east of the Adriatic and Ionian seas; Cephalonia, Zante and Cerigo guarded the vital route to Crete and Cyprus, and a vigilant supreme officer, the *provveditore di Levante*, stationed at Corfu, had overlord's powers of swift action in the region. The Turks were watched, if not walled in, by the formidable line of fortresses and shipping flying the banner of St Mark, militant symbol of the affluent Christian west.

Until 1570, a peaceful balance was preserved, apart from the war which broke out because of a mistaken action at sea in 1537. The Turks' invasion of Corfu and its dependent territory in this war (1537–40) was fearfully destructive, but their siege of Corfu did not succeed, and they gained in the end only Monemvasia and a number of Venetian places still remaining in the Aegean region: Nauplia with its territory, and the islands of Aegina, Mykonos and the northern Sporades. Provided the Turks continued to believe that the Venetians were strong, and the Venetians were prepared to pay tribute, it did not seem that conflict was inevitable. The danger lay in unpreparedness and short-sighted parsimony. Cristoforo da Canale, in his dialogue *Della Milizia marittima* (written in the 1540s), pointed out the folly of not spending heavily enough on fortifications and warships; a speaker in the senate in 1569 emphasized the same points, when fear for the safety of Cyprus arose. There were also appeasers who wanted to explore the possibility of paying higher tribute for the island, seeing in this only a tradition which went back to the payments made long before by the Lusignans to the Mamluk sultans in Cairo. Cyprus was lost in the war which broke out the following year, but even this loss was partly redeemed by the Turkish defeat in the battle of Lepanto (October 1571): this showed that offensive retaliation

50

34 Trireme from Cristoforo da Canale's *Della Milizia marittima* ▶

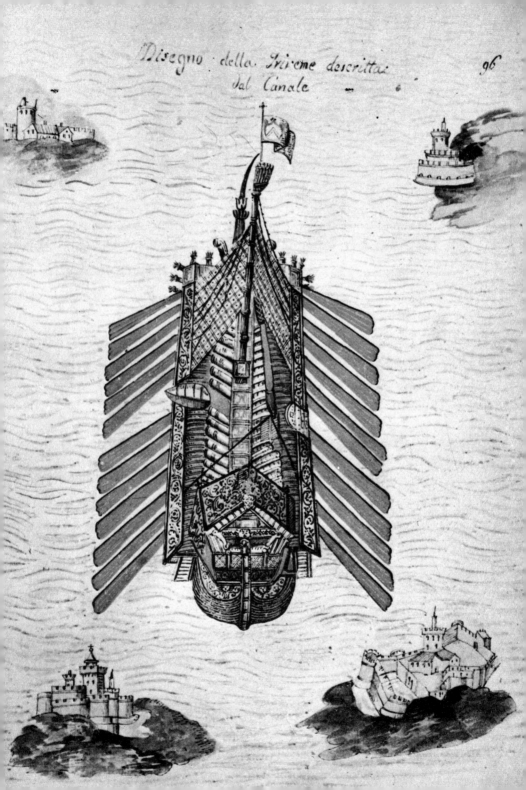

could be effective – the Venetians resumed their policy of 1201–04 by involving themselves with a powerful 'crusading' alliance.

In such a brief review of the empire *da mar*, focus has had to be placed on its foundations of trade, and then upon its fortunes in the presence of Ottoman power. Little has been said about economic productivity and settlement in the Venetian dominion overseas or about imperial administration. The inscription which Marin Sanudo noticed upon the walls of Pirano in Istria in 1483 – 'Behold the winged lion! I pluck down earth, sea, and stars . . .' – might suggest that the régime was uniformly and mercilessly rapacious, but in fact it would seem to have been neither.

That the Venetians 'exploited' their dominions economically hardly requires to be said: the empire has already been defined as essentially a commercial enterprise. Surplus agricultural produce could only be exported to or through the metropolis: Cretan wine and corn, for instance, or, in the sixteenth century, the raisins of Zante and the olive oil of Corfu. It would probably be wrong, however, to see this in general as expropriation and profiteering by ruthless Venetian landlords, driving and depriving Greek peasants and serfs. The biggest settlement had been in Crete in the thirteenth century, but in the second half of the fourteenth the wealthiest planter aristocrat of Venice was reputedly Federigo Cornaro, with his great sugar-producing estates in Cyprus, which was not then in the Venetian empire at all. Not enough is yet known about the colonial wealth of Venetian patricians, whether resident or absentee, but odd islands or estates in Crete and Negroponte were not necessarily Eldorado. Guglielmo Querini was a patrician of middling fortune who inherited lands in Crete and the small island of Gozi, and some of his correspondence from 1428 to 1461 survives. In letters to his cousin Filippo, who represented him in Crete, Querini complained that in fourteen years of possession his only advantage from the estate had been a small wine cask, and that Gozi was difficult to resettle because of the terror of pirate raids. On the other hand, Andrea Barbarigo (1399–1449), who had two cousins with large estates in Crete, did good business as their agent selling produce such as cheese, wine and kermes dye, and his sons benefited more from inheriting these estates than they did from Andrea's own bequest.

Administratively, Crete was again the most thoroughgoing colony, with its institutions directly modelled upon those of Venice. The duke of Candia, with his cabinet of two councillors and another official called the 'captain', were all Venetian patricians elected at home and appointed for short terms by the central government; there was also a Cretan *maggior consiglio* and senate composed of settler patricians. The leading officials of the Venetian empire were always patricians appointed in Venice, apart from some of those in charge of local dependencies of an individual dominion. The governor's title varied from place to place: bailiff (*bailo*) in Negroponte and Corfu, count in Zara, governor (*luogotenente*) of Nicosia in Cyprus; rector, prefect or castellan in many smaller places. Specialized officials were more regularly called *capitano* (in charge of defence), *podestà* (justice) and *camerlengho* (revenues). But existing customs in civil jurisdiction and land tenure were generally maintained; as late as 1451 a new edition of the *Assizes of Romania*, the civil law code of the Latin empire of Constantinople, was completed for use in Negroponte. In many of the Greek, Slav and Albanian communities, some degree of participation in government was also allowed. In Corfu and Cyprus, for instance, this even extended beyond the usual confinement to a patrician caste; but participation was always limited to the locality concerned, or its immediate dependencies, and a Venetian senator's proposal in 1411 that the nobility of Zara should be eligible to take office elsewhere was, for example, repulsed immediately. More will be said in a later chapter about public relations, but the guiding principles of the imperial administration during this period were not rigid but pragmatic: maintenance of Venetian defence, communications, commerce and revenues came first, then support of whatever elements could be best expected to ensure peace and stability. The 'soldiers of the sea' were only thus far 'new Romans'.

THE ITALIAN MAINLAND

Even more striking than the increase of overseas dominion in the period after 1380, was the increase of direct Venetian rule upon the *terraferma* of Italy. Within the previous 200 years many independent cities and despotic rulers, most recently and spectacularly the Visconti of Milan, had expanded their dominion in the northern half of the peninsula, but no 'free commune' or republic did so on the scale of fifteenth-century Venice. In 1463 pope Pius II shared the Florentine view that the Venetians' ambition was to subdue all Italy, and although he thought this would be almost impossible for them to achieve, he conceded he would welcome it as an alternative to subjection to the Turks. Niccolò Machiavelli, less an admirer of Venice than so many of his fellow Florentines, expressed in his *Discourses* (*c.* 1515–20) the haunting suspicion which had become so common in the course of the fifteenth century, that the Venetians had been aspiring to 'a monarchy of Italy like the Romans'.

Appearances tell, even if the interest of the Venetians in the Italian mainland expressed no sudden ambition to gain territory, revenues and jurisdiction, but was more concerned with the security of traditional lines of commerce: the exchange of 'spices' and other goods for German metals, and the protection of markets in north-east Italy. In the thirteenth century, Venetian dominion on the mainland had not extended beyond a strip bordering the lagoon known as the 'Dogado'. The situation was rather similar to that overseas: direct political dominion was limited, but Venetian patricians acquired estates subject to other lords, and special privileges and jurisdiction might be conceded to resident Venetian merchants, as for instance they were in Ferrara.

On the other hand, in the fourteenth century inland rulers who were obstructive or predatory about the passage of goods to and from Venice through their territory, provoked the republic to war and annexation. In 1339 the outcome of a long war against the della Scala, rulers of Verona, was the acquisition by Venice of Treviso and its subject province, from Mestre on the lagoon to Conegliano in the Alpine foothills. After 1380 a much greater concentration of hostile forces led to further extensions of the mainland empire. The unreliability of Padua as a neighbour under Francesco I da Carrara (*signore* of Padua 1350–88) had been proved by his hostilities in the Genoese war of 1379–80, his ambitions in Friuli and his intrigues even further afield in Corfu. For two years Padua passed from the rule of Francesco's son to the even more formidable dominion of Giangaleazzo Visconti (lord of Milan from 1385 to 1395, thereafter duke until 1402) who had also appropriated the della Scala cities of Verona, Vicenza and briefly reoccupied Treviso. Yet more mainland enemies surrounded Venice: the patriarch of Aquileia, with his extensive lordships in Friuli and Istria, and the king of Hungary, since 1386 Sigismund of Luxembourg, who denied the Venetian rights in Dalmatia.

After Giangaleazzo Visconti's sudden death in 1402, the Venetians acted quickly. By 1405 Vicenza, Verona and Padua had all admitted Venetian lordship; and when Visconti power rose again under Filippo Maria, who annexed Genoa in 1420, the distant cities of Brescia (1426) and Bergamo (1428) were taken by the Venetians in the first phase of a long war in central Lombardy, which later brought the vital link of Peschiera (1440) and the distant city of Crema (1447). War had also been declared in 1411 against the patriarch of Aquileia and against Sigismund, king of Hungary and by then also Holy Roman Emperor, who claimed that the mainland cities acquired by Venice belonged to Imperial jurisdiction. The outcome of decisive Venetian victories was that by 1420 the patriarch's enormous jurisdiction had become Venetian, and so too had the mountain cities of Feltre and Belluno on the upper reaches of the river Piave, and Rovereto on the river Adige, all commanding important routes over the Alps; finally, in 1437, Sigismund even conceded Venetian rights in Dalmatia.

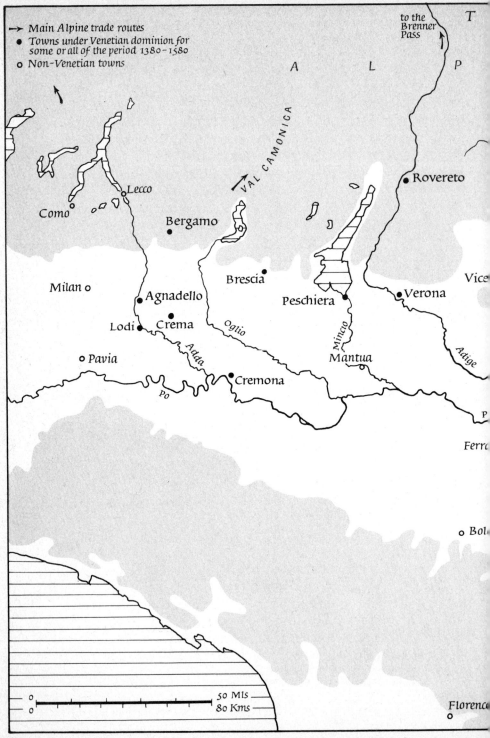

→ Main Alpine trade routes
● Towns under Venetian dominion for
  some or all of the period 1380–1580
○ Non-Venetian towns

T

to the
Brenner
Pass

A   L   P

VAL CAMONICA

● Rovereto

Como ○

Lecco ●

● Bergamo

Milan ○

● Brescia

Peschiera ●

● Agnadello

Lodi ● ● Crema

○ Pavia

Oglio

Adda

Minico

Mantua ○

Vice

● Verona

Adige

Po

● Cremona

P

Ferr

○ Bol

50 Mls
80 Kms

Florence ○

35 Venetian possessions and communications in north–east Italy, 1380–1580.

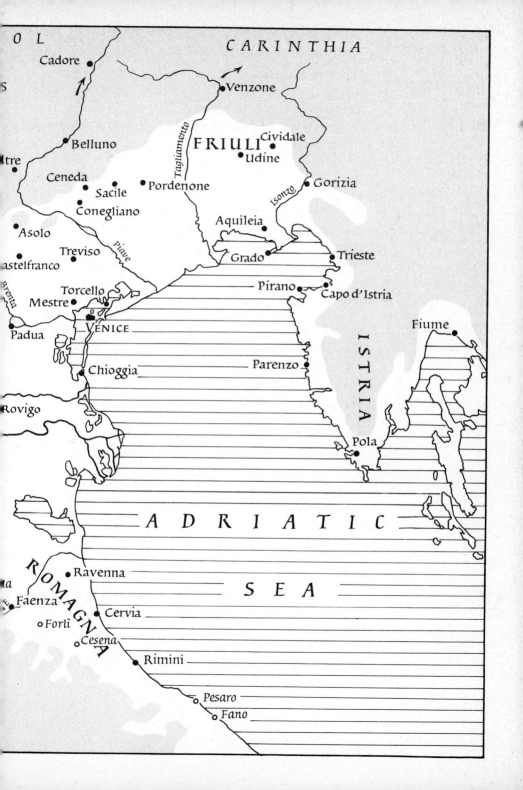

The rapid building of this Italian empire, in 1423 already stretching from the hills behind Verona to the Julian Alps, was acclaimed by doge Tommaso Mocenigo in his famous speech to the senate (1423). The dying doge saw it as the basis for a golden future in terms of rising capital investment in trade: not as a policy of territorial ambition for its own sake, which he considered was the dangerous wish of the favourite candidate to succeed him, Francesco Foscari. Mocenigo would certainly have thought little of historians' judgments that there had been a deliberate retreat to dry land by the Venetians, alarmed by the growth of Turkish power in the east; there was no inconsistency for him between the old empire *da mar* and the new one *da terraferma*. For Foscari, in spite of the taunts of irresponsibility, there was probably little difference either. With Visconti power rising again, the republic could hardly have refrained from taking the offensive and investing millions more ducats in the mainland campaigns which brought the western frontier within twenty miles of Milan.

At the time, no other Italian power objected greatly to a Venetian expansion which robbed the della Scala, da Carrara, Visconti, and that obsolete ecclesiastical prince, the patriarch of Aquileia. The papacy and the Florentines had for long been promoting alliances in the name of liberty against those who supported the eagle of the Empire and the viper of Visconti Milan. Compared to these long-established symbols of voracity, the winged lion was a newcomer, welcomed into alliance by the Florentines in 1425. Concern arose later, from the uncertainty of Venetian objectives. Where would they stop? Would they be content with what had always been their sphere of interest, or continue to expand indefinitely? Alarm in Italy became serious after Filippo Maria Visconti died in 1447 without an heir, when the city of Milan declared itself a free republic and some of its subject cities voluntarily ceded to Venice. Did the Venetians covet Milan? If so, their pretensions might cover all the former dominion of the Visconti, far beyond Lombardy, into Piedmont, Liguria and Tuscany.

It is impossible to be certain about ultimate Venetian objectives. Policy in Venice was decided collectively and proceeded more on an *ad hoc* than a long-term basis, and thus the Venetians themselves were probably uncertain. Undoubtedly there were jingoists and intransigents in the senate, while others considered the best way of securing and extending Venetian interests was by unprovocative diplomacy and co-existence. Francesco Barbaro (1398–1454) gave his advice as an enlightened patrician in 1447, that an alliance with the post-Visconti 'Ambrosian Republic' was the best means of subordinating Milan to Venetian influence; much the same policy had been attempted in the previous century with the client state of Padua under the earlier da Carrara, and was usually pursued towards the Gonzaga of Mantua. Barbaro stated the alternatives: 'whether to increase our empire or increase common liberty and the peace of Italy. The credit will be much greater for Venice to appear as the supporter of Italian liberty.'

Fear of Venice was nevertheless great enough for Cosimo de' Medici to direct Florentine foreign policy in a quite new direction, breaking the alliance of the two republics which had reputedly been protecting the liberty of Italy since 1425. From 1452 to 1454 Florence was at war with Venice, Cosimo supporting the claim to Milan of Francesco Sforza, Filippo Maria Visconti's mercenary captain and son-in-law, who was recognized in 1454 as ruler of a reduced Visconti dominion. A major aim of the Peace of Lodi, signed in that year, and of the Medici-Sforza alliance, fundamental for the quiet of Italy for the next forty years, was to check Venice. Writing in the next century, the Florentine historian Francesco Guicciardini still judged that it was this which prevented a Venetian lordship of the whole of Italy.

Events to some extent justified such suspicions of Venetian policy in Italy, though there was no lack of self-righteous indignation to refute them. Paolo Morosini, who wrote an articulate description of Venetian government (1464), also composed the elaborate *Defence of the Venetians to the Princes of Europe against their Detractors*, dedicating it to the Venetian cardinal Marco Barbo. He maintained that Christian duty and self-preservation activated the republic, and certainly the offensive mainland policy seems to have been concerned only with the traditional areas of Venetian interest: eastern Lombardy, Friuli, the Po delta and the coasts of 'the gulf'. The trouble was that these were districts about which both Florence and the papacy were highly sensitive, on account of their own territorial interests.

The risk of provocation had already been taken in 1441 when Ravenna, claimed as a papal city *de jure*, but long governed by the da Polenta family, lapsed to Venice by a deed of inheritance; it became acute again in 1463 when the Venetians negotiated to buy Cervia, with its valuable salt-pans. Malatesta Novello, the seller, was a vassal of the Church, and the pope denied his right of alienation. Pius II lapsed into an even more bitter diatribe than he had emitted over the Congress of Mantua or the war in Morea. According to his own account, he not only told the Venetian ambassador, 'Your cause is one with thieves and robbers,' but launched into prophecies of doom:

No power was ever greater than the Roman empire and yet God overthrew it because it was impious and He put in its place the priesthood because it respected divine law ... you think your republic will last for ever. It will not last long. Your populace so wickedly gathered together will soon be scattered abroad. The offscourings of fishermen will be exterminated. A mad state cannot long stand.

The 'mad state' did in fact survive worse papal censures than this, and its robberies continued unrepentantly. The climax of mainland 'imperialism' came in the last two decades of the fifteenth century and the first few years of the sixteenth. The first occasion was the war which pope Sixtus IV provoked in 1482 against the kingdom of Naples; despite Pius II's invectives, he even tempted Venice into alliance by the promise of ports in Apulia and some territory of the marquis of Ferrara, who was technically a papal vassal. But the pope, alarmed by the forces he had provoked, soon tried to go back on this; by the following year he had not only sponsored a league against Venice, insisting particularly on a naval expedition against the city, but also imposed an interdict. Nevertheless, with the unexpected support of Ludovico Sforza of Milan, in the final peace of 1484 Venice retained the Polesine of Rovigo, a fertile tract of territory north of Ferrara. The Polesine had been in Venetian hands for nearly half a century after 1395, as security for a loan to the then marquis; it had been handed back in 1438 only on condition of through access. Even so, the republic had acted high-handedly, as arrogantly as it was acting at the same time in the east over the Ionian islands and Cyprus, and as it continued to do in the following years.

The foreign invasions of Italy, beginning in 1494, were the great stage upon which the last acts of Venetian empire-building were played. A more heroic performance was applauded: it was claimed that during this long crisis Venice displayed a true concern for the independence of Italy and vindicated itself as the new Rome. There was some truth in this, but it was greatly exaggerated. For the curtain rose upon a murky scene: over ten years earlier, when the Ferrarese war was going badly for them, the Venetians had encouraged Charles VIII of France to make good his claim to Naples; and even in 1493–94 his overtures were not at once rejected. These included the promise of Apulian ports and Greek lands in return for active support in the east, where he hoped to proceed like a new Charles of Anjou.

Resistance to the French occupation of Naples, demanded by king Ferdinand of Aragon, was at last resolved early in 1495. The Venetians had no wish to see a new French presence in the east, or provoke the Turks unnecessarily, quite apart from their alarm at the disturbance to Italy. A defensive league was signed in Venice itself on 31 March, and the Venetians took much of the credit for creating this alliance, patronized by the pope, the Emperor, king Ferdinand and the duke of Milan. As their pledge for a loan, they helped themselves to Trani and several other

Apulian ports, and forces in their pay were present at the battle which Charles's retreating army faced when it descended the eastern slopes of the Apennines (Fornovo, July 1495). The Italian losses of men were much greater than the French, and the Venetian divisions of the army did not acquit themselves with much glory, the *stradiotti* or light cavalry of the empire *da mar* having disobeyed orders and looted the baggage-train. Nevertheless, it was celebrated as a Venetian victory, whereupon doge Agostino Barbarigo, who had not been present, was hailed by Sanudo as 'the new Augustus'.

Such credit to Venice was, however, rather tarnished four years later. Alarmed by the Visconti-like pretensions of Ludovico Sforza, and his entertainment of a Turkish ambassador, the republic entered into alliance in April 1499 with the new king of France, Louis XII. Probably Louis's claim to the duchy of Milan was expected to lead to a long, inconclusive war weakening Sforza power, while Venice held the balance, and to a French presence in Italy which would be just as transitory as past invasions. Instead, the French were quickly victorious, and the Venetians made the best they could of the situation by taking Cremona as their reward, extending their frontier to the river Adda and even claiming (unsuccessfully) Lodi, Lecco and other places on its further bank. There was a strong element of *sauve qui peut* in this crisis, which saw so much of Italy fall suddenly under French occupation. But more Venetian miscalculations followed; it must have been assumed either that Louis XII would keep faith, and that his concurrent alliance with the papacy would not turn to the republic's disadvantage, or that Venetian strength and subtlety would be more than a match for him.

It was in the region where the papacy was so sensitive, and which had provoked Pius II's frenzied abuse of 'the mad state', that the gathering danger lay. Pope Alexander VI was not prejudiced against Venice; in 1502 he was trying to impress upon Venetian ambassadors the need for a Venetian-papal league 'for the conservation of your own interests and of

Italy'. 'Your power is great, but you alone cannot dampen this fire,' he declared. But upon his death and the disintegration of his son Cesare Borgia's principality, the Venetians instead kindled new fire by offering their protection in Romagna. Marin Sanudo expressed in his diaries the righteous arrogance which determined Venetian action. 'We all know the intention of the [doge's] council, which is to have the Romagna if we can, and seize it from the hands of the duke Valentino, this enemy of God and ourselves.' Though less successful at Cesena, the Venetians took possession of Russi, Forlimpopoli, Rimini and Faenza in November 1503; their power now extended to the foothills of the Apennines. The Venetians justified themselves by the local encouragement they received as protectors who would restore order; their ambassador in Rome declared, 'if Cesena wants to come under Venetian rule it is because the latter is just and beneficent'. Girolamo Priuli (1476–1547) commented less confidently in his diary, 'perhaps it would have been better not to snatch at every passing fly'.

The Venetian *terraferma* was now extending to a hinterland which seemed beyond the traditional spheres of Venetian influence; Forlì, Imola and other towns would be claimed next. The new pope, Julius II, who as a cardinal had been friendly towards Venice, could not tolerate these incursions into territory so recently acquired by Cesare Borgia and which he was determined to regain for the papal state. The basis of a hostile alliance against Venice had already been laid at Blois in September 1504, although for the time being the pope was prepared to negotiate about the Romagna, since he first wanted a free hand to capture Bologna. Julius II's relations with Venice deteriorated further over appointments to bishoprics in the *terraferma* and other issues of ecclesiastical jurisdiction. A story is told by Luigi da Porto (1485–1529) about a discussion of such matters between the pope and the Venetian ambassador Giorgio Pisani. Julius ranted that he would not rest until the Venetians were again humble fishermen, and Pisani replied, 'Then we will easily make you a poor parson [*un piccol chierico*] if you are not careful.' The story may not be exactly true nor the issue so immediate a cause of war as da Porto suggests, but it illustrates the sort of irritation which was hardening Julius against Venice. The immediate pretext for the alliance was the final phase of Venetian land-grabbing, this time at the expense of the Emperor Maximilian. Refused permission to pass through the *terraferma* with an army on his way to be crowned in Rome, Maximilian had replied with hostile invasions of Venetian territory in the spring of 1508. His forces had to retreat on all fronts, while the Venetians took possession of Trieste and Fiume by naval assaults, seized the independent enclave of Pordenone and rounded off their dominion in Friuli with the county of Gorizia. When the Venetians made a three-year peace with Maximilian without consulting Louis XII, who in theory was still allied to them, all their enemies drew together.

No independent Italian state had ever faced such a formidable combination of European powers as the League of Cambrai, which declared war against the Venetians in December 1508, on the pretext of their 'insatiable cupidity and thirst for dominion'. Had they really been so insatiable and resolved on the subjection of all Italy? Many observers for over half a century had thought so, nor was it considered against the interests of Italian independence to call in foreigners to fight Italian battles. Even in October 1504, with both French and Spaniards in the peninsula, the opinion had been voiced in a Roman banquet that it was the lesser evil to be dominated for a time by barbarians: these would pass like others before them, while from Venetian rule there would never be escape.

Yet in practice Venetian policy had remained inconstant, as it was bound to do because of the frequent changes of persons responsible for it. Occasions for aggrandizement had been missed, and generally the Venetians were too wary to violate Imperial and papal lordships. Mantua and Ferrara were coveted but not seized; they were all the republic claimed to want, much less a wider share of Italy, when approached by French ambassadors in 1500. To avoid a collision with the pope, Venice

36 Allegory of the war of the League of Cambrai by Palma il Giovane. Doge Loredan confronts Europa with the militant justice of Venice and a snarling lion of St Mark (Padua is seen in the distance). Painted *c.* 1585.

remained so tolerant of Cesare Borgia's advancing power that in 1502, for instance, Senigallia, Pesaro and Ancona were refused protection. No serious attempt was made to subject any of the western seaports of Italy, apart from some military aid to Pisa in its war against Florence. Such restraint is remarkable in the face of the extraordinarily vindictive alliance of the League of Cambrai, which expressed all the mounting fears of Venetian quasi-Roman ascendancy. The four most majestic names in western Christendom, pope Julius II, Louis XII, Ferdinand of Aragon and the Emperor Maximilian were its signatories.

The war of 1509–17 has never been called the 'Great War of Venice' – so much else came to be involved in it – but this name would not be inappropriate, considering that the aggressors' initial purpose was to carve up the Venetian land empire, and

65

that the outcome was the restoration of most of it to the Venetians. In a way, the fact that the alliance was so heavily weighted against them was the Venetians' good fortune. If it were to succeed, combined operations were needed, and these were difficult to organize. Meanwhile, Venice was able to pose as the injured martyr of Italian independence; in the earliest military actions against the French, troops in Venetian pay are reported to have shouted 'Italia!' as they entered battle.

The recovery and triumph of Venice has less hold upon the imagination, however, than the calamity from April to June 1509. Papal forces took the Romagnol cities and after the French victory on the Adda at Agnadello (14 May), there seemed to be a total lack of will to resist as the enemy advanced to the river Mincio, and a loss of nerve in the capital. Even the diaries of Venetian patricians express disillusionment. Marin Sanudo declared that if he had been in the senate in May 1509 he would have proposed sending ambassadors to the Ottoman sultan to ask for aid. Girolamo Priuli, whose fortunes as a private banker were almost ruined by these events, denounced the doge and senate as unworthy of their ancestors: their panic suggested that the king of France was encamped on the banks of the lagoon, instead of a hundred miles away at Peschiera.

O great and famous Romans [Priuli wrote], O Marcus Curtius and infinite other Roman nobles, who exposed their lives for the least danger to their country, how deservedly their glory and fame will last for ever, and the Venetian senators are not to be compared at all to these holy Romans, as I chose to call them for the glorious experiences they saw and the deeds they did. And the Venetian fathers are not worthy to govern such a republic on their present showing.

The recovery of Venice, slower and less spectacular than its apparent collapse, lay in devious diplomacy which took advantage of the League's disunity, in provincial reactions against the invaders and in the enduring power of Venetian wealth, trade and empire overseas. Had the capital also been threatened, this recovery might not have been possible, but Venice itself remained secure. Fortunately, the Aragonese fleet did not follow seizure of the Apulian ports by sailing up the Adriatic; most of the papal army remained in Romagna, while the French, most formidable of the allies, stayed in their allotted share of the Venetian dominion, west of the river Mincio. Maximilian did not arrive at all until August. The Emperor's delay was the Venetians' opportunity. By ordering submission to his representative, the renegade Leonardo Trissino of Vicenza, they appeared to abandon some of their own cities in the nearest part of the *terraferma*, the region which was allotted to Maximilian by the League; but by so doing they deprived the French of a pretext to advance, and bought time in which reactions could develop against Trissino. This worked so well that the most important city, Padua, was regained in July, and Vicenza returned to St Mark in November. On the other hand, Imperial forces retained Rovereto and Verona, and though Maximilian's long siege of Padua failed in the late summer of 1509, his forces recaptured and sacked Vicenza the following June. Meanwhile, in Friuli there were heavy Venetian losses, and some of the most loyal elements turned to the Emperor in 1511.

But the prospect was never again so desolate as it had seemed in June 1509. Venetian diplomacy succeeded in dividing the League. At the cost of many concessions, the loss of Ravenna and the Romagnol towns, the Venetians were able early in 1510 to make a separate peace with pope Julius, whose alarm at the foreign presence in Italy was easily inflamed. With Spanish and English support, the weight of alliance turned into a 'Holy League' against the French, to the rallying cry of 'Out with the barbarians!': much to Maximilian's embarrassment. The Venetians' opportunism was blatant, for not only did they make a truce with Maximilian in 1512, but the following year they deserted this league to make an alliance with the much weakened French. This was taking a great risk, and after French defeats in 1513 Spanish cannon even fired across the lagoon from Mestre. But it succeeded when the French were again victorious under Francis I; at the Peace of Noyon in August 1516, the French-occupied parts of Venetian territory, excepting Cremona, were restored. The following year Maximilian, the most dogged but least efficient of the belligerents of Cambrai, was persuaded to renounce his claims for 60,000 ducats, though he retained Rovereto.

Machiavelli disparaged Venice in his *Discourses* and *Florentine History* for its apparent collapse in 1509; he chose to make light of Venetian resilience although at the time he had (according to a dispatch from Verona) been impressed by provincial loyalties. He professed in these later literary works that Venice was finished; likewise, his friend Francesco Vettori compared the republic to a man dying of consumption. Yet even if military ardour had been lacking, no other Italian power save Venice had pitted such courageous astuteness against force, Petrarch's *virtù contro al furore*, which was the panacea Machiavelli himself recommended for Italy in the final chapter of *The Prince*. Apart from Ravenna and Rovereto, the final losses were only those places most recently and most provocatively acquired: the Romagnol and Apulian towns; Cremona; Trieste, Fiume and the county of Gorizia. Priuli may have been right in judging his fellow patricians as unequal to Roman heroes, but another saga in the 'new Roman' mythology of Venice lay in this survival against heavy odds; and in spite of the defeat of Francis I at Pavia in 1525, Venetian territory was not subject like the rest of Italy to the Emperor Charles V.

True, there was little prospect of revived Venetian expansion. Although Ravenna was briefly regained from 1527 to 1529 during the papacy's troubles after the Sack of Rome, and Venetian diplomacy succeeded in re-creating a Sforza 'buffer state' of Milan for a few years, the illusions of the century before 1509 were lost. A Venetian ambassador, who quoted Charles V saying in 1529 that he did not want a universal monarchy but he knew others who did, thought he was referring to the Venetians; he must have been a purblind ambassador, either to have been so blimpishly out of date, or to have missed (if the Emperor had indeed meant the Venetians) what could only have been a touch of irony, at a time when Charles could not afford any further war in Italy. Nevertheless, the saner fulfilment of Venetian interests, a large regional empire of *terraferma* in Italy, survived and flourished in the sixteenth century: its population was reckoned as nearly two million by about 1570.

In many ways this mainland dominion, which doge Tommaso Mocenigo had seen as only a guarantee of the wider commercial empire of the Venetians, was similar in its administration and development to the dominion overseas. It was even dependent upon naval power: during all the land wars Venetian fleets travelled up the river Po and its tributaries. In the campaigns of 1439–40 when Brescia was besieged by the Milanese forces, a fleet was dragged across the hills behind Verona and launched upon Lake Garda; armed barges defended the river Isonzo against Turkish overland raiders in 1477.

Government followed much the same pattern, with Venetian patricians appointed for short terms to the highest administrative offices, and a great variety of pragmatic concessions allowed to preserve continuity where this made the régime more stable. The instructions to Andrea Zulian, sent to the newly annexed city of Brescia in 1428, were perhaps disingenuous: 'Adopt gentle words, so that all are content with our dominion, and declare to them that we only claim customary dues and taxes, and ask them if they are so disposed to accept our rector, or prefer to elect their own consuls dependent on the republic.' But at least a certain amount of civic autonomy, including fiscal rights and courts of first instance, was allowed, and if civic institutions were generally preserved for the local patricians to run, there was no single system of election imposed on them, nor of exclusion imposed on others. In the former lands of the patriarch of Aquileia, participation in the civic government of Udine was more 'open' than in most other cities, while in Cividale it was dominated by the rural nobility, and the 'estates' or parliaments of Friuli continued to meet.

Fiefs were held of the Venetian republic in this border region and the mountain valleys behind Brescia and Bergamo, rather as they were in the Aegean islands; mercenary captains who deserved well of Venice were often the beneficiaries: Bartolomeo Alviano, for instance, was invested with Pordenone after its capture in 1508.

The taxation and customs revenues from this enormous mainland province, including the rich cities of Brescia and Padua, certainly enabled the Venetians to pursue their grander projects overseas and to maintain their prestige as a great power. Priuli justly restated the 'Mocenigo doctrine' that from the maritime state proceeded the profit and honour of Venice, and defeatists in 1509 understood by this that the misfortunes of Venice arose from disregarding the ancient ways and that the best hope lay upon the sea alone. But the *terraferma* was the essential complement to the empire *da mar*, as doge Mocenigo, and Foscari after him, had clearly intended, and a speech to this effect was made by Alvise Molin before the senate in the dark days of July 1509. The version of this speech reproduced by Luigi da Porto in his history written in the form of letters is doubtless inaccurate, but its imagery of 'the most delightful, populous, and fertile part of Europe . . . the flower of the world acquired and maintained by our ancient grandfathers and ourselves with so much effort', does not sound too far-fetched; nor do its challenges: where overseas could such a splendid dominion be found, such a safe market for Venetian salt, spices and other goods, such a source of abundant revenues? Summarized estimates of Venetian revenues in the fifteenth century confirm that the net income to the state from the *terraferma* was about twice as much as that of the dominions *da mar*.

Economic exploitation of the *terraferma*, as of the empire overseas, must be understood in only a limited sense. There is little evidence of a sudden 'flight' of Venetian capital into land as a result of the mainland annexations in the fifteenth century. Some of the confiscated Carrara lands near Padua were bought by Venetian patricians, and the fashion for acquiring (mostly small) mainland estates, near enough to Venice for a short visit, and productive enough to meet a family's needs in food, was undoubtedly growing in the fifteenth century; but it might just as well have occurred without political dominion.

The affairs of Guglielmo Querini and Andrea Barbarigo provide examples. Querini possessed a small fief in the Polesine, under Ferrarese not Venetian jurisdiction, which yielded modest amounts of fruit, wheat and wood; but, like his Cretan estate, it was far less important to him than business speculations as an import-export merchant. Barbarigo increased his modest fortune from 1600 ducats in 1431 to perhaps as much as 15,000 by 1459, mainly by traditional trading ventures in pepper, English cloth, Syrian cotton and Spanish wool. He lived in a rented house, and although he bought a small estate near Treviso in 1443 this was a holiday home rather than an income-bearing investment.

On the other hand, property may have been regarded as a safe investment when the prospects of trading profits were poor. It was in this spirit that Andrea's son, Nicolò Barbarigo, drew up his will in 1496, advising his sons to preserve an estate near Verona and to be wary of commercial ventures. But this was not a doctrine intended for all times and circumstances: Venetian money was invested in mining and other industrial enterprises on the mainland, and manufactured goods had to be exported through Venice, though these could be counted as benefits as much as exploitation. Crops were not requisitioned, but Venetian landowners were obliged to sell in Venice in times of scarcity; and in the sixteenth century money was invested heavily in agricultural improvements, irrigation and drainage. Quotas were placed upon cattle for the Venetian meat market, but mainland stock-breeders successfully resisted or reduced them. The estates, revenues and patronage of mainland bishoprics and religious houses under the control of Venetian patricians probably provide the biggest example of 'exploitation' following annexation: the secular empire was generally more restrained.

y coumence la descriptio
ou tractie du gouuernemet
et regyme de la cyte z seigne
de venise. Prologue.

C'est escript au
premier liure
des Roys au cha
pitre xv q me
lior est obedie
ta q victime.
C'est adire q mieulx vault obeis
sance que sacrifice. Et cor Il me
sort comade que Je mette en es
cript le Regime de venisiene
C'est adire comat la seignurie
de venise gouuerne Icelle cyte z
aussi les aultres cytes z lieux
qui sont soubz la Juridition
de lad seignurie. Laquelle char
ge en soy est fort difficile et a
mor par plussieure Raysons
quaf impossible. Car tous les

aucteurs de liure tant anciens
que modernes ont trouue plus
grant difficulte a declarer le gou
uernement des prouinces z les
Regimes des cytes que a descrip
re simplement les histoires mars
come on vort par experience plu
sieurs pour ceste cause des gou
uernemene et Regimes ne sont
point de mention. Et se aul
cune se sont mise a faire telles
descriptions de quelque petite
prouice et maindre cyte que ce
sort. On peust coprendre clair
ment par les stille z maniere
descripre quilz nont peu si facille
ment declarer ce q par les ma
tiere subiecte estoit dit ou adi
re. cor Ilz ont fait ce aultres par
tie de seurs tracteurs et liures.
Il fault aussy cosiderer la chose
publique de venise estre bien

III VENETIAN GOVERNMENT

38 Medal proclaiming
patriotic unity
between senate and
greater council, c. 1457.

That the Venetian constitution was near-perfect came to be commonly believed in the imperial age, as did the fiction that Venetians were new Romans. Even in the thirteenth century St Thomas Aquinas had praised it as a mixed and temperate polity; in the fifteenth century one might choose between Poggio's praise of it as Cicero's ideal of true aristocracy, or George of Trebizond's belief that it was Plato's ideal of a mixture of monarchy, oligarchy and democracy. 'The Greek republics did not last more than 450 years, the Roman seven hundred, and this one has already lasted more than a thousand,' Bartolomeo Moro declared before the greater council in December 1516, 'and the cause is the concord: and so it will be until the end of time.' In fact, the subject of Moro's speech was the corruption, particularly the misappropriation of funds, which had prevailed in Venice for the past twenty years; even in the context of criticism he deferred to the convention of praising Venice as a perfect state.

In Giannotti's *Dialogue on the Republic of the Venetians*, written in 1525–26, another patrician, Trifone Gabriel, is made to disavow the comparison between himself and Cicero's friend Atticus, notwithstanding his retreat from public life to a country villa, 'because the Roman republic was corrupt, and my republic is not'. Not all Venetian patricians were self-deceived. Girolamo Priuli even went to the opposite extreme in the malicious criticism which his private diaries contain. Certainly the Venetian system of government lasted, and during this period was served by a remarkable number of able men, but it was only relatively stable, concordant, peaceable, just, uncorrupt and possessed of all the other attributes of perfection so

73

◀ 37 The doge, possibly with the council of ten (and assiduous citizen secretaries), as depicted in a late fifteenth-century manuscript by an unknown Frenchman: an example of foreign interest in Venice and its institutions.

often claimed for it; and the mystery of how it held together cannot be explained by any simple formula.

Perhaps no one but a contemporary statesman, a doge or procurator of St Mark's nearing the end of a lifetime of public office but not yet in his dotage, could have explained properly how the government worked, with its multitude of magistracies and councils: what were the special qualities which enabled a patrician to make his way to the top, what influence or graft, what calculated seizure of opportunities were needed, or how private interests bore upon collective decisions. Many treatises upon Venetian government in the late fifteenth and sixteenth centuries describe the skeleton, but none succeeds in animating it with flesh, blood and brains.

The Venetian system bore little resemblance to any other known: a republic with its head of state, the doge, elected for life from a closed corporation who formed the membership of the greater council, and monopolized hundreds of lesser offices. According to Paolo Morosini in c. 1460, there were 2000 of these privileged individuals, representing 150 family names; according to Marin Sanudo in 1513 membership had risen to 2622. Over 800 jobs had to be filled, most of them for short terms; over two-thirds of them were magistracies which functioned within the city of Venice itself; about 150 were concerned with the mainland empire; another hundred or so were appointments overseas, including foreign embassies and galley commands, with various additional offices in time of war.

Higher appointments and resolutions of policy rested with the smaller assembly which assumed the neo-Roman title of 'senate' at some undetermined time in the fourteenth or early fifteenth centuries; it had about 200 members, the larger proportion elected annually by the greater council, the rest taking their places *ex officio*. The senate, with its consultative 'college of sages', including the five *savi grandi*, five *savi ai ordeni* for maritime affairs and (since about 1420) five for the *terraferma*, together with the council of ten, which had special responsibilities for security, held extensive and growing authority. The

39 Bertuccio Contarini's sworn admission to serve as a procurator of St Mark's (1485). Left, the arms and status-conscious device of the Contarini.

supreme lordship of Venice (*serenissima signoria*) consisted of the doge and his cabinet or lesser council (*minor consiglio*) of six elected councillors, together with the three acting heads of the criminal appeal court. But the essential base of the pyramid was the greater council, the patricians' corporate body.

The extraordinary character of this ruling caste needs to be dwelt upon, for the male succession in a limited number of families determined all the political life of Venice. Between 125 and 150 family names were represented, but many of these privileged dynasties contained a large number of collateral branches: for instance, no less than 39 members of the greater council in 1512 bore the name of Contarini. It would be wrong, therefore, to assume that blood was always thick, or relationship near among all patricians with the same surname; nor were

75

all who bore a particular family name entitled to sit in the greater council; the surname might have been acquired from unqualified ancestry, or conferred by favour. Right of membership could also be confiscated because of disgrace. Legitimate birth was very carefully checked: in 1506 the special register of patrician births known as *The Book of Gold* was begun. Giovanni Bembo, writing a memoir in 1536, recalled the anxiety lest his son, born long after betrothal but only nine days after he married his Greek wife from Corfu, might have been disqualified. However, as this example shows, the patriciate was not 'closed' on the maternal side; one of its sources of strength was that wives did not have to be patrician daughters.

Their status as nobility was a rather tender subject for the Venetian patricians. Twelve families who claimed their ancestors had taken part in the election of the first doge, and another twelve who claimed distinction before the year 800, believed themselves to have a greater nobility than the rest. Yet for all the heraldic arms and honorific forms of address, the truth could not be hidden that the status of the patricians derived not from land and papal, Imperial or royal patents and titles, but solely from the recognition of the Venetian régime. The words *patrizi* and *gentilhomeni* were used to describe them as often as *nobeli*, and in an age when the nature of nobility was a favourite topic of scholarly discussion, the Venetian patricians' only hope lay in definitions depending on long-standing respect, or in some cases riches and virtue. Poggio may have changed his views about them, but Machiavelli sceptically repeated how unlike they were to any other sort of nobility; Pius II, himself born of an impoverished Sienese noble family, scathingly complained that he did not know whether their arrogance rose from 'inveterate pride or the rudeness inherited from their fishermen ancestors'. All this may help to explain the craving for pretentious Roman genealogies, the relative concord and the self-congratulatory patrician praise for the system of government, upon which not only their political and economic privileges depended, but also their social dignity.

In Venice there was also a sub-patriciate, consisting of those with the status of 'citizen'. Citizenship could be acquired on a basis of prolonged residence, non-manual occupation and financial means, and there was an *élite* of families in the citizen grade known as 'original citizens'. Citizens of long standing might even be allowed the privilege of engaging in overseas trade. Notaries and permanent civil servants were members of the citizen class; they could rise to some prominence as secretaries of the council of ten or of the senate, serve in resident embassies or secretaryships abroad or through a career in the chancery attain the dignity of grand chancellor of the republic; thus they might possess much secret influence and knowledge of affairs. Though they had no chance of a political career, no vote in the greater council, citizens were allowed a gratifying measure of respect. They were part of the 10 per cent of the population distinguished from mere inhabitants or plebs, towards whom the patrician attitude was expressed by Gasparo Contarini (1524): 'All hired labourers and artisans ought to be regarded as public servants.' Citizens might be as boastful as patricians about the régime. Pietro del Monte, a Venetian humanist friend of Poggio, was one who, in spite of having no political rights, professed he was 'brought up in the strongest fortress of liberty and had never felt the harsh yoke of tyranny'.

If citizens could be rich and patricians poor, records suggest that, in proportion, the patricians had by far the greater share of wealth invested in trade and interest-bearing loans to the government. As their detractors commented, there was never any shame about investing money in trade for a Venetian patrician. In fact business experience was considered one of the assets of a potential statesman. Girolamo Priuli, a great-nephew of two doges, declared in his diary: 'My father, proud of his native country and its liberty, did not spare himself day or night in finding ways of making money . . . business is a good thing for the public economy.' Patriotism, family pride, caste solidarity and the wish to fulfil Ciceronian ideas about the duties of the active life, may all have inspired the patriciate to

77

dedicate themselves to public affairs; but individual business opportunities were also enhanced by such activity.

There were selfish advantages in being a Venetian patrician, but also drawbacks. In his caustic essay *On Nobility*, Poggio wrote, 'I would rather be Apuleius' ass than a Venetian nobleman', referring to the supposed intellectual limitations and concern for trade of the nobility, but the image of the ass might more appropriately suggest burden-bearing than stupidity. To spend every Sunday afternoon in the council hall, operating the intricate balloting procedures upon which the election to offices depended, cannot have been exhilarating. No analysis has been made of the distribution of offices over a given period, but only a minority of patricians could expect to rise above the lower grades. Service in the city magistracies might bring financial reward in the form of a proportion of the revenue from fines imposed, but the hours (especially for the magistrates who had to patrol the streets at night) might be arduous; while service outside Venice, or even self-maintenance in the dignity of a senator, would require the use of private means. Attempts to evade office, particularly ambassadorial office, were well known in the fifteenth century, whether by negative canvassing in the greater council (urgent messages of 'Don't elect me! Don't see me!') or fabricated disqualifications such as debt or temporary absence on business. That membership of the greater council was not altogether enviable may even have been one reason why the system continued to go unchallenged; perhaps the excluded class felt they were better off outside it.

The relative secrecy in which Venetian government was conducted helped to preserve the appearance of harmony. Even for a patrician of the greater council, it was often difficult to discover what was decided at higher levels: Girolamo Priuli, who was frank and critical, on paper at least, complained that one had to depend on gossip. Senators were subject to a vow of secrecy about current proceedings, which must have been deeply frustrating to foreign ambassadors, with the result that their dispatches from Venice are usually much less informative

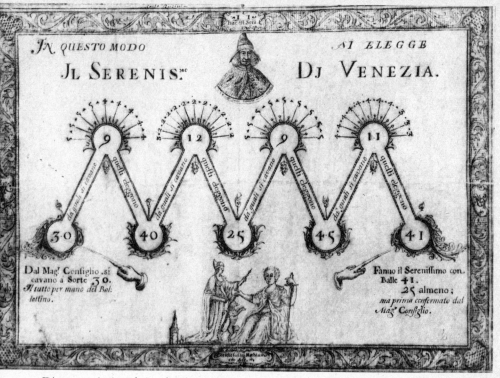

40 Diagram (printed in the late seventeenth century) showing the traditional procedure for forming the electoral college to elect a new doge.

than those from other cities and courts. Sometimes it appears that secret contacts could be arranged. Evidence that this sort of disloyalty occurred lies in the scandal of 1405, when it transpired that various patricians (including the naval hero Carlo Zeno) were being paid by the Carraresi of Padua. It is difficult to find out whether such bribery was widespread. The ambassadors of Ludovico Gonzaga, marquis of Mantua, wrote of cordial friends in high places, to whom they referred by code names. Domenico Luciano described how he waylaid such friends in the street; Ludovico de Gratego boasted in February 1470 that many senators were his friends, including the acting head of the council of ten. But the whole business was shrouded in secrecy and peril, unlike the easy listening-posts and doors to high places in other centres of diplomacy, such as the court

79

of Rome, where the Venetians were so adept at penetrating secrets and speculating on policy, making themselves the best-informed diplomats of Europe. Legislation on secrecy became increasingly severe; in 1481 it was enacted that no member of the senate or governing councils should speak of affairs of state to ambassadors or other foreigners either in his own house or elsewhere, under a penalty of 1000 ducats and two years' exile.

Outsiders might easily have gained an impression of concord in the political life of Venice, but it would be incredible if the patriciate had not been bitterly divided by their personal and family rivalries, differing attitudes, interests and financial means. The difficulty lies in detecting the ways discord found expression. The official records of senate and greater council proceedings are brief and omit what was said in debate; chronicles, particularly Sanudo's so-called diaries, covering the years 1496 to 1533, tell more, but selectively. Sanudo's own political career was constantly frustrated by powerful groups whom he does not name; he may have been resented as a too outspoken critic and prying historian, or as a man of too modest means.

The allocation of public funds almost invariably provoked opposition. To give some random examples, in 1451 a proposal to pay the *podestà* of Bergamo 1400 ducats was carried in the greater council against an opposition of 275 votes, with 81 more undecided (*insinceri*). The following year even a proposal to order the construction of a new state galley for the Alexandria route, in place of one which was unseaworthy, was opposed by 17, with 13 undecided; a slightly larger number opposed the majority who were to vote a suitable reward to Gentile Bellini for his mural decorations in their own hall in 1474. Disagreement within the assembly, even if fractious, was no sign of disruption, but there were also cabals which intended much greater harm to the system. In 1432 as many as twenty-three patricians were incriminated for swearing on the Gospels to help each other accumulate offices; in 1517 Sanudo records similar intrigues. Paolo Paruta (1540–98) gave up active political life altogether, allegedly because he found the struggle to be elected and the intrigues too intense and demoralizing. The identification of those who supported the forces of discord and their motives for opposition are as yet unknown, and it will never be possible to unravel fully the tangle of family relationships, investment interests and personal prejudices which governed the attitudes of the patrician body. Three groups of discontented patricians may be quite clearly recognized, but they do not form very coherent political forces.

First, there were the 'poor patricians'. Sanudo tells of certain humble offices being reserved for them: two ushers (*apontadori*) at St Mark's and the Rialto who had to ensure that all officeholders were in attendance at the right time each morning, and eighty sinecure pensions called *poveri al pevere* given in reward for service overseas to patricians who faced an impoverished old age. Perhaps it was the poor patricians who voted in opposition to heavy state expenditure, but it would not seem they were likely to present a serious problem in terms of subverting the state. They might try selling their votes or interest, and in 1517 Sanudo reveals there was a group of less affluent senators who were derisively nicknamed 'the Swiss' for this practice. On the other hand, the poor patricians, including the lazy, stupid and apathetic as well as those ruined by hard luck, might be those least likely to bother about turning up at meetings of the greater council, unless this was a vital psychological consolation to them in their ruined condition.

Another source of discord within the patriciate is suggested by the division into old or 'long', and new or 'short' families. The twenty-four early medieval dynasties who regarded themselves as the authentic nobility were the 'long', and the rest were 'short'; both despised those newcomers whose right to sit in the greater council dated only from the 1380s. It may have been an expression of fear or jealousy among the 'short' patricians that after 1414 no doge was elected from any of the 'long' families until the seventeenth century; on the other hand, it is surprising that such exclusion had not occurred in the fourteenth century if the majority feeling against all the 'long' families was indeed so bitter. It is not clear that degrees of patrician antiquity mattered very much in normal politics. Only sixteen different family names out of the possible total of just under 150 are represented in the dogeship between 1414 and 1570. Thus the absence of the 'long' might have been by chance, though admittedly very few of the 'long' became procurators of St Mark's in this period. Scurrilous remarks were made when Andrea Vendramin became doge in 1476, his family being one of those admitted after the war of Chioggia (see p. 24), but part of the explanation may lie in jealousy of his excessive wealth. It is difficult to see what differences in policy and public interests the relative pride in ancestry could provoke, and the rise of 'new men' could hardly provide a basis for conflict in Venice as it could in Florence, since there were virtually none.

Perhaps more troublesome than either the rich-poor or ancient-modern divisions within the patriciate was the division between the younger members and the old. The youthful David was not a heroic figure in the Venetian republic as he was in Florence; Solomon was a far more appropriate symbol under a system which reserved higher responsibility to the middle-aged, and the highest dignities of all to the elderly. Of the twenty-three doges between 1400 and 1570, the average age at election was seventy-two; the three youngest were the exceptional Francesco Foscari (forty-nine) in 1423, Alvise Mocenigo (sixty-three) in 1570, and Leonardo Loredan (sixty-five) in 1501. The large number of patricians under forty and therefore debarred from the senate, or even under thirty and debarred from many functions including the election of a doge, might well have been discontented with such a gerontocracy. Admission, with voting rights, to the greater council was officially fixed at twenty-five, but every year thirty young men over the age of twenty were admitted by ballot on the day of the Feast of St Barnabas; entry even at the age of eighteen was allowed upon payment of 20,000 ducats from the time of the League of Cambrai crisis. Thus in any year there might be at least 150

41, 42 Two 'young' doges: Francesco Foscari (1423–57) and Alvise Mocenigo (1570–77).

patricians under the age of twenty-five in the greater council, and many more not yet forty.

The young patricians were not afraid to criticize their elders. Girolamo Priuli was scathing about his great-uncle, doge Agostino Barbarigo, during whose rule he entered the greater council (1498), and castigated doge Leonardo Loredan and the whole senile régime in 1509; 'they valued their own lives as though they were immortal, yet they had no certainty of living even one year longer, most of all on account of their great age'. Equally, the seniors regarded the juniors with caution and mistrust. Francesco Foscari had been considered a dangerous 'young' man (at the age of forty-nine) to become doge. In 1583 the French ambassador reported that such was the licence of the young men that the patricians believed it would eventually become insupportable. Yet the discontent of the young patricians was not so much subversive as inspired by a more zealous conservatism and patriotism than that of their elders. The young were usually the warmongers, resentful of diplomatic compromises such as produced treaties with the Turks in 1503, 1540 and 1573, and the constitutional purists, resentful of the grasping power and secrecy of the council of ten, which even interfered in foreign policy. They were not inclined to make any fundamental changes to the social and constitutional framework within which their opportunities lay. Nor were they discontented through idleness. If they were excluded from the senate and high office, they were eligible to serve as one of the five *savi ai ordeni* and they staffed many of the lesser magistracies within the city – night patrol duties or the many different species of customs and excise offices, for instance. In fact, the magistracies open to young men of twenty-five or thirty were the very ones most gratifying to the exercise of petty power, involving day-to-day contact with citizens, artisans, plebs and foreigners, reassuring the young patrician official of his privilege and detachment since he personified the authority of the Venetian republic.

At its most accessible and trivial levels, the Venetian state was operated not so much by the grey-haired as by officious youths, and conflict may have risen more from the apprehension of the old at being outclassed than any disrespect of the young for their sacred institutions. When in 1510 the senate lowered its age of admission to thirty for a limited number of places, conditional on large loans to the public funds, it was objected that such young senators would be less able to preserve secrecy; but this was overruled, and according to Priuli, the young senators were rather better than their elders in guarding their tongues. An earlier diarist, Malipiero, mentions an episode of 1478, when a fall of plaster from the ceiling interrupted a session of the senate, and three patrician youths were found to have been listening above to the oration of the ambassador just back from the Ottoman sultan. But these eavesdroppers were only sixteen years old; called before the council of ten, they were released to the mercies of their parents.

84

43 *Promissione* sworn by doge Leonardo Loredan after his accession (1501). Doges were obliged to swear to a covenant of good behaviour and constitutional rectitude ▶

Serenissimus Princeps: et Excellentissimus Dominus Domin. Leonardus Lauredanus

deivoce Inclytus Dux Venet. 20 tang patronus: et uerus guber
nator ec̄: et Capelle sue S. marci decreuit et b̄ene conuenie
ntibus respectibus: et causis hec edere Inuiolabilit̄ obseruanda ab Ca-
nonicis suis vz:

Quando eius subl.mus processio cum Cap.lo S. marci proficiscetur duo
Cancellarij eius Inferiores: si surrexerit quis esset Cano. S. marci no
uadant cum Cap. Sz precedendo an personam S.s sue. Indutj tamen
uestitus non sacris neq̄ cota. Comitet̄ dnum Cancellarium Vene
medius inter eos: et ob hoc non amittant porcionem suam Cano. no secus:
ac si sacris uel Cota Indutj cum Cap. precederet

Item q̄ in processionibus que fiut tam singulo die mercurij q̄ prima
dnica mensis cuilibet: et rogationum et. Sacristes Celebraturus
missam sacris Indutus, omniū ultimus ueniat. Precinit et uz. S.
marci Dmistris Secum. et inter eos Immediate precedet Diaconus:
et subdiaconus Sacris Indutj an quos uadant dicto Cancellarij Infer
iores: et eradum alij digniores Cano. secundum tempus assumpnois sug:
Ita q̄ omnes Cano. p seipsos: et non p alium psona debere teneatur
missas Comitiales: et uesperas secundum q̄ eis p tabellam tetigerit
non excipiendo quepiam: nec etia Cancellarios Inferiores Saluo semp. iusto
Impedimento presente sub pena soldoi uiceti pro qualibet uice: et si

If such divisions existed within the patriciate, they were not really deep enough to destroy the image of serenity which Venetian ambassadors, known to be responsible and accountable to the senate, portrayed to the outside world. Foreign powers could hardly exploit them in any significant way, though the Emperor Maximilian tried to do so during the League of Cambrai war. He addressed an open letter to 'the commune of Venice', meant to stir up not only non-patrician citizens, but also the 'long' patrician families. It began with the statement that, 'the good fathers of the ancient nobility with dexterity, prudence and a certain sound moderation founded, increased and conserved this state of Venice, at present oppressed by the young and the collective new nobility'. The Emperor claimed that he had taken up arms so that Venice should no longer be suffocated in this way: 'Place yourselves again beneath the sceptre of the Holy Roman Empire and the true ancient nobility.' Such obvious propaganda, designed to reduce Venice to the level of one of the Imperial free cities in Germany, had little hope of succeeding and it is not known whether the letter was ever received. Not only were patrician resentments insufficiently strong to be attracted by it, but the allegations were ridiculous. Admittedly the doge, Leonardo Loredan, was a member of a 'short' patrician family (i.e. one of those which had risen after the ninth century, but before the fourteenth) but one of the heads of the council of ten was Girolamo Querini, of a family which belonged to the 'true ancient nobility' of the seventh and eighth centuries, and many of the senators belonged to these families. The 'oppression' of Venice was a massive joint enterprise by the ancient as well as the less ancient families, by the old as well as the young.

THE DOGE: IMPERATOR AUGUSTUS

Though all the patricians of the greater council were involved in the government of Venice, both city and empire, the living symbol of authority, union and concord was the doge. His importance should not be underestimated. Prior of the collective lordship or *signoria* of Venice and supreme magistrate, he was elected by the most complicated of all balloting procedures, in an electoral college of forty-one patricians of the greater council. There was never discontinuity in the office, since the oldest councillor of a deceased doge took over his responsibilities during a vacancy.

A patrician who became doge of Venice tended to be an elderly and wealthy careerist who had already reached a summit of ambition by becoming one of the nine procurators of St Mark, the honoured life trustees of property endowed to the saint and of all other testamentary bequests. A Milanese ambassador wrote scornfully in 1478 that for the patricians 'to exhaust themselves in all these elections is not very necessary, because these doges are not of great moment. For they elect a life associate [*socio*] rather than a duke.' By the despotic standards of Milan, perhaps, a Venetian doge might appear a mere figurehead of the patriciate, but for those who believed in republican government, moral strength lay in rulership which could not become arbitrary. Bernardo Bembo wrote in his commonplace book, 'All the princes of Italy are tyrants except for the doge of Venice.'

There was, moreover, a great aura of sacred or imperial majesty about the first magistrate of the Venetian republic. Crowned with a horn-shaped biretta, enthroned according to an elaborate liturgy, escorted in public processions beneath the ceremonial umbrella authorized by the pope in 1177, the doge had no equal in grandeur among the lay princes of northern Italy. Pope Pius II was even warned by the scare-mongering Florentine ambassador in 1463 that, 'either the apostolic eminence will be destroyed entirely or the Venetians will arrogate it to themselves and unite it with the dogate'. True, the doge was a salaried and accountable official; he could not give judgment or even receive ambassadors on his own; he was a prisoner, unable to leave Venice at his own wish; he could be made to abdicate, like doge Foscari in 1457, or his wish to abdicate could be refused; this happened to Foscari at earlier stages in his career, and also to doge Agostino Barbarigo in 1501 and to Francesco Donà in 1550. But if the doge was judicious and able, respected as an elder statesman of long-standing experience and influence, his will would surely command deference and carry weight with his councillors and the senate and council of ten: it seems likely that in practice he could determine policy.

Even if the patricians imposed elaborate restrictions upon the office, and made the doge on his accession swear an oath (the *promissione*) to observe a rigorous contract of good behaviour, they were unable to curtail the numinous prestige which lingered, or rather increased, during this imperial period. Although a law passed in 1401 had decreed that the doge should be addressed as *messer* rather than *dominus*, the grandiose style which prevailed was that of 'most serene prince'. Literary acclaim for doge Agostino Barbarigo as 'Augustus' and 'Prince of the New Rome' has already been mentioned; Francesco Negri, a Dalmatian Slav who sought his fortune in the imperial capital, dedicated his treatise on the greatness of Venice, *De*

44 Procession of dignitaries, including the doge, in the Piazza San Marco;

Aristocratia, to doge Barbarigo first and then to doge Leonardo Loredan as 'Most Serene Prince, most illustrious Duke of the Venetian Aristocracy and Periarchon of its most sacred Senate'.

As the British monarchy, in the most imperial period of the nineteenth century, still retained deference and considerable power in spite of constitutional restrictions, and even gained a new aura of romantic majesty, so did the Venetian dogeship in the fifteenth century. The successes of Venetian arms and diplomacy were associated with the individual doges who presided: Michele Steno, Tommaso Mocenigo and (for the earlier part of his career) Francesco Foscari. Equally, of course, the doge's prestige suffered in adversity; the flamboyant princely style of Foscari was all very well in the years of victory against Filippo Maria Visconti, but it declined to ignominy when the outcome of so long a period of mainland war was a restored Milanese state supported by Florence, and in the east when Constantinople and other Greek cities were seized by Mehmed the Conqueror, one of whose informers was allegedly the doge's own nephew, Jacopo.

from a woodcut of the sixteenth century.

45 Doge Agostino Barbarigo and lions beneath the sun of justice. The sculptor's inclusion of the ceremonial sunshade (conferred upon doges by papal grace) makes the allegory slightly ambiguous.

But the conception of the doge as *imperator* remained compulsive. Even Foscari's successor, the diffident doge Cristoforo Moro, was in the end persuaded to play the part of a new Enrico Dandolo and take the cross in 1463; although Moro's career as a crusader came to nothing more than a trip to Ancona, the election in 1474 of doge Pietro Mocenigo continued the militaristic trend. Mocenigo had been the naval commander who tried to retrieve Venetian fortunes after the fall of Negroponte; he had his tomb decorated with the epitaph, 'From the booty of enemies', and a standing figure of himself beneath an arch was surrounded with warriors, trophies and scenes representing his own somewhat inflated 'triumphs'.

It was doge Agostino Barbarigo, however, who exceeded all others in the new style of princely pomposity. This is clear from his reconstructions of the doge's palace, with the great staircase designed as a summit from which the doge might inspire awe at coronations and receptions, and the decorations within his own apartments, which included his own monogram and devices such as the one of himself and two lions basking beneath the sun of justice. Girolamo Priuli wrote in general terms about

46 Tomb of doge Pietro Mocenigo (d. 1476) by Pietro Lombardo. The doge's martial fame (he is even wearing armour) provides the general theme; the relief carving on the bier depicts the Venetians entering Smyrna in 1471, and the handing to Caterina Cornaro of the keys of Famagusta.

47, 48 Medal struck during the reign of doge Foscari.

the dogeship in the early sixteenth century, that in spite of what was said about its being 'like a signboard outside a tavern', in fact the Venetian prince could do a great deal. 'Should the prince want to do something against the interests of the republic he will not be supported, but for the rest, truly in the smallest things, he can do what he likes so long as it does not harm the honour and decorum of the state. Whoever would contradict him has to proceed very cautiously.' About Barbarigo, however, Priuli commented, 'He did whatever he wanted and with this imperiousness placed all his friends and servants in office without deliberation; no one was able to contradict him. At weddings or on return from public appointments all went first to do the prince reverence.' He even expected his hand to be kissed.

Doge Agostino Barbarigo had no doubt taken advantage of the times, but after the loss of Modon (for which he was reviled) and his death soon afterwards in 1501, there were repercussions. Inquiries revealed not only that he had sequestrated money, which his son-in-law was made to repay, but that he had been involved with his brother Carlo in smuggling large quantities of wine to avoid duty. In vain Marin Sanudo demanded that the new Augustus should be spared this posthumous disgrace, that the scandal should be hushed up and hearings restricted to the council of ten. Instead, 1200 patricians attended the greater council to listen to these sordid revelations, and Sanudo feared, 'even the mechanics will hear everything, bringing great shame upon the state'.

Fortunately for them, Barbarigo's successors, particularly Leonardo Loredan (1501–21) and Andrea Gritti (1523–38), restored the dignity of the dogeship in their long tenures of office. Loredan may not have been quite so incorruptible and sagaciously calm as Giovanni Bellini's portrait suggests; in 1505 a lampoon appeared, depicting a female Venice weeping to St Mark and the text, 'I don't care, so long as I grow fat, I and my son Lorenzo', and Loredan's apparent inertia during the initial calamities of war in 1509 was also criticized, even if his refusal to go to Verona and inspire resistance may have been

49 Commission of doge Andrea Gritti to his namesake Andrea Gritti as count of Sebenico (1534).

50 'The Most Serene Prince': Giovanni Bellini's portrait of doge Leonardo Loredan.

judicious, and his sons perfectly correct in their assurances, 'The doge will do what is best for the country.' Sanudo remarked that Loredan was 'more dead than alive', and Priuli noted his ill-disposed state of mind as well as his poor health. Nevertheless, Loredan lived for another twelve years, and luckily for his reputation, presided over the recovery of Venice. After his death, there was a similar inquisition to that held in 1501, and little was found to discredit him. Andrea Gritti, who had been an intrepid diplomatist at Constantinople during the Turkish war and a hero of resistance to the Emperor's siege of Padua in the crises of 1509, also avoided the more extravagant vanities of the late fifteenth century. The wild ride of the Barbarigo dogeship had raised discord to an alarmingly high pitch, but it was not repeated, and its failure was to be symbolized by the placing at the head of the great staircase of Jacopo Sansovino's enormous statues of Mercury and Neptune (1566). Personifying patrician force and wealth, these figures reduced the dogeship to scale.

93

'The principal foundation of our city and its singular ornament is justice, both at its heart and in its subject lands.' These opening words of a motion before the greater council in 1435 express one of the proudest Venetian claims and explanations of their envied concord. Aristotle's highest political virtue, impartial justice, was what the Venetian state was supposed to represent to the world; this was even more important than the nature of its constitution, a true aristocracy or a fusion of the best political systems. 'That natural stronghold of the state, the faith of the people, is best retained by justice', Alvise Mocenigo wrote sententiously in his relation of 1546.

The doge's palace, as the principal seat of justice, was adorned with images representing this. A female holding up an enormous sword, seated between two lions (just beneath the throne) and above the crushed figures of rebellion, was carved in the fourteenth century upon the thirteenth roundel of the loggia on the piazzetta façade; on the capitals of the lower storey were the heads of exemplary figures such as Aristotle, Solon, Scipio, Numa Pompilius, Moses and Trajan. A Florentine sculptor carved (c. 1430) the Judgment of Solomon on the corner of the palace nearest St Mark's; the new entrance to the palace, the Porta della Carta, was surmounted by Bartolomeo Buon's figure of Justice, with sword and scales, seated on a lion (1441); the top of the waterfront façade received a standing Justice with scales in 1579; so did the piazzetta façade.

Much was admirable about the civil and criminal jurisdiction of Venice. The laws allowed a patrician to plead no privilege, much less exert any private jurisdiction; courts of first instance were devised to be accessible and speedy, and there was an elaborate system for appeals. Yet how justly it all worked in practice is uncertain; the subject is vast and little investigated.

There are certain cautionary points which have to be set against adulation. The regular procedures in criminal justice were always subject to citation of a case to the summary jurisdiction of the council of ten, which allowed the accused

51 Justice: the figure by Bartolomeo Buon placed above the Porta della Carta, entrance to the doge's palace and its law courts. The figure originally stood against the sky ▶

no defence or appeal. The verdicts in lower courts might be swayed by the practice of paying the magistrates a percentage of the fines they imposed, in criminal cases, and on the values at issue in civil suits. The absence of patrician privilege did not mean the absence of patrician prejudice; since all magistracies were restricted to members of the greater council, some degree of this was almost inevitable. It might sway judgment and produce lenient sentences. For instance, a few years of exclusion from office was the punishment for those patricians treasonably implicated with the Carraresi of Padua in 1405. Nicolò da Canale, who had the greatest responsibility for the loss of Negroponte in 1470, and Antonio Grimani, who failed to save Navarino and Lepanto in 1499, seem to have escaped rather mercifully, by comparison with the ruthless sentences imposed on Carmagnola and other mercenary captains who failed to acquit themselves well; Grimani even lived down his record to become doge for two years (1521–23). Patrician influence was obviously used to cancel the heavy penalties imposed on Jacopo Sansovino after his first building for the Library of St Mark's had collapsed in 1545. Finally, the Venetian penal code varied strangely between humanity and violence, from fines or temporary exile to crude tariffs of mutilation and execution. Lombard rather than Roman ancestry seems to lurk in some of these judicial barbarities. In 1454, for instance, Ettore Soranzo and Andrea Surian had their right hands cut off just for placing more than one ballot ball in a voting urn of the greater council.

Nevertheless, even Pius II admitted, 'within the memory of our fathers Venetian justice was rated very high', and one can hardly take seriously his invective about its sudden degeneracy over the illegal purchase of Cervia:

What do fish care about law? As among brute beasts aquatic creatures have the least intelligence, so among human beings the Venetians are the least just and the least capable of humanity, and naturally, for they live on the sea and pass their lives in the water; they use ships instead of horses; they are not so much companions of men as of fish and crowds of marine monsters.

52, 53 Two popes who attacked Venice: left, Pius II (1458–64); above, Julius II (1503–13).

These fish-like subhumans of Pius II's imagination had none the less contrived a system which aspired to do justice much more effectively than that of the papal state. Impartiality and accountability were implied by the elaborate machinery of short-term appointments and collective judgments; for even the judges of the appellate courts were non-professionals elected from the greater council, and their verdicts were reached by voting. The same system of appeal in civil cases, whereby the appellant first referred himself to one of the auditors of the court, was extended as far as possible to the empire *da mar* and *terraferma*: special auditors or *sindaci* were sent on circuit at regular intervals, so that those who sought justice were saved the expense of coming to Venice. When Marin Sanudo accompanied the *sindaci* round the *terraferma* in 1483, he related that

97

they were formally instructed to set forth displaying 'humanity and a smiling face', and that public proclamation of their presence was made in each place they visited. Since the *sindaci* normally sat in session with Venetian officials serving in the locality, it may be that courage was needed to present an appeal or complaint even by common petition; and if the *sindaci* were convinced by the allegations of injustice, they still had to refer the case back to Venice, which might take a long time. Cases may have been dismissed, either at the initial or ultimate stages, thanks to patrician solidarity against abusive criticism.

Nevertheless, maladministration was sometimes proved and led to dismissal and punishment. For instance, in 1431 Secondo Pesaro, one of the councillors of the duke of Crete, was fined 796 ducats and sentenced to two years' imprisonment for taking bribes and for other offences; in 1503 Troilo Malipiero, captain of Famagusta, was deprived of office for three years and banished from Venice for his oppressive government; no less than three rectors of Aegina were disgraced in the sixteenth century. In such inaccessible outposts of empire Venetian justice was least dependable; in Lepanto, for many years before it fell in 1499, the administration had been neglectful, permitting the oppression of inhabitants by the local nobility. Many abuses no doubt went undetected, but at least there was some provision for, and some instances of, a Venetian Verres being rooted out.

Patricians whose minds were touched by humanist teaching professed not only the ideal of impartial justice, but also the idea that virtue lay in the active political life, that the highest moral duty was imposed by their privileged birth. Zaccaria Trevisan, captain of Candia (1403–04), was described by the humanist scholar Guarino as a shining example of 'Latin prudence and Greek amiability'; in 1407 Trevisan wrote to his successor in another post, the captaincy of Padua, 'The special traits of a Venetian governor are a sense of humanity and clemency, to make yourself loved, whereas other lords rule citizens from the heights of their citadels.' In 1417, Francesco Barbaro, perhaps the most distinguished of all the Venetian

54 Guarino of Verona.

patricians befriended or taught by Guarino, sent to Sante
Venier, count of Zara, a copy of Cicero's letter to the proconsul
Quintus, exhorting the count to study ancient authors since
this assisted one to perform one's duty to the republic. Barbaro
himself set an example of stoical devotion to duty as *podestà* of
Brescia, during the siege of Milanese forces in 1438–40. No less
assured of his political virtue was Ludovico Foscarini, *podestà* of
Verona in the years 1451–52, who wrote: 'I study government;
I want to compose quarrels; I ponder about the amenities of the
city; I favour the poor; I do not fail to do justice; I am willing for
all to be heard and judged by me.'

Doubtless many Venetian officials fell far short of the bene-
volent proconsular mystique (and perhaps one should say self-
conceit) of Trevisan, Barbaro and Foscarini; one has to balance
it against the rather hysterical allegations of Girolamo Priuli.
Patrician greed for more and more offices and magistracies was,
according to him, one of the main reasons why Venetian
dominion was extended so recklessly; the number of jobs had
to keep pace with the still rising numbers of the greater council.

Their 'scant justice and overbearing pride' led to the divine vengeance of 1509. However, even Priuli admitted that some Venetian magistrates were worthy, and he was proud enough of his own father's record as *podestà* of Cremona, member of the council of ten and holder of many other offices.

At least there is some evidence of a conscientious paternalism and concern about public relations on the part of the Venetian patriciate, and the enthusiasm for governing well was certainly fortified by the Roman associations of Venetian territory, and the sense of belonging to a revived Roman civilization. On his journey with the *sindaci*, Marin Sanudo remarked on the Roman walls and theatres at Verona and Pola, and copied down modern inscriptions commemorating recent Venetian governors as zealously as if they had been antique; he followed Sabellicus in writing an account of Aquileia and Friuli as the 'Tenth Province' of Roman Italy. The benefits of living under this empire were quite considerable, since they included the rule of law, the provision of defence, assured communications, markets and consumer goods, with the well-supplied city of Venice itself as an ultimate refuge in trouble.

One benefit it did not confer, however, which differentiates it so much from the Roman precedent, was equal political citizenship. In Venice itself, relations between the patricians and the politically ineligible classes, citizens and plebs, were seldom troubled by this inequality. Not even after the crisis summer of 1509 did sufficient tension arise to threaten the constituted order. A certain current of resentment among the citizens that they were being overtaxed, and that the patricians ought to pay for their own war, was apparently silenced by clever patrician tactics. Early in October, many citizens were summoned into the hall of the greater council (a gracious concession which itself probably won half the battle) and treated to an eloquent and disingenuous harangue by Antonio Loredan. He argued that it was they, not his own patrician order, who were the truly privileged class in Venetian society. As civil servants they enjoyed life tenure, as merchants they could concentrate on making their fortunes; the patricians, on the other hand, had only temporary appointments in government, heavy expenses and the risk of losing their lives as officers in time of war. 'We make do with the odour of the state, and you eat the roast meat; we bear the name, and you the prizes; we the leaves, and you the fruit.' Whether or not these were Loredan's exact words, the desired effect was made.

Meanwhile, the Venetian artisans and plebs seem to have been just as docile as the citizens. Some of the economic and social reasons for this will be discussed later, but it is remarkable that not even the large concentrations of manual labour in the city, the Arsenal and the fishermen's quarter of San Nicolò, presented a danger to the patrician régime; in fact they were staunch loyalists, with a traditional trust associating them with the doge in particular as bodyguards. For the *arsenalotti*, there was regular employment and perquisites including free wine, even if a day's wages might be lost occasionally by failing to clock in on time, or if their foremen dealt out corporal punishment. There were occasional demonstrations, such as the march on the doge's palace of 300 armed Arsenal workers in 1569, demanding payment for the time spent collecting their wages on Saturday afternoons, but they were exceptional. Whatever the rest of the artisan population, retail traders and craftsmen thought about their exclusion from active citizenship, they were not at all vocal about it. To plan and co-ordinate a rebellion in Venice would in any case have presented enormous physical problems, as Tiepolo's attempt in 1310 had proved; the elaborate system of custodians for each ward, heads of neighbourhoods and parish informers, also had to be reckoned with.

In the Venetian empire, both *da mar* and *terraferma*, it was different. On the one hand, the artisans, smaller tradesmen and peasantry seem generally to have welcomed Venetian rule as a lesser evil than unrestricted urban oligarchy or oppression by either native or Venetian landlords. Far away in central Lombardy, the rural commune of Palazzolo had preferred direct subjection to Venice in 1428 than to Brescia, the city in whose rural district (*contado*) it lay; in the other direction, Marin Sanudo noted in his itinerary of 1483 that the inhabitants of Ceneda had applied to have a Venetian patrician as their *podestà* rather than be subject to the neighbouring jurisdiction of Sacile. This does not mean that there was no rural *jacquerie* under Venetian rule, and in the early summer of 1509 the peasants round Padua thought more of seizing land for themselves than of defending their government; nevertheless, in mainland towns and countryside a mob could usually be trusted to turn out shouting the pro-Venetian slogan, 'Marco! Marco!' at crucial times.

On the other hand, there was some discontent among those who considered themselves worthy of the highest citizen rights on the *terraferma*. Social historians have been inclined to over-generalize about this discontent. Much of the evidence for it comes from the quite abnormal conditions of the League of Cambrai war, following nearly a century of peace for most of the Venetian dominion. Taxation had been increased in recent memory for war against the Turks; now there was not only taxation, but total insecurity of life and property. The many local patricians and citizens aspiring to patrician status, who were prepared to be neutral or collaborate with the invaders, may have felt in their bewilderment only a relative rather than a fundamental hatred of the Venetian régime. The slogan scribbled on city walls, 'Light has dawned among the shadows', the release proclaimed at Padua from 'the yoke and servitude of Pharaoh', grossly distorted the true state of affairs. Padua may present a special case, where there were many whose ancestors had suffered a more ruthless dispossession by the Venetians than elsewhere. Yet the largest of 'the shadows' had been cast by local forces; civic régimes were becoming confined to certain families long before the Venetian conquest, and Venetian influence in Verona, for instance, was used to try and broaden rather than narrow the ruling patriciate. This may not have been enlightened; the purpose was probably to make the latter weaker or more servile, and restraint was imposed on elements known to be anti-Venetian. To save local taxpayers, however, the central government attempted in the late fifteenth century to limit expensive provincial embassies to the capital, and if the superior jurisdiction of Venetian magistrates and officers was resented, this grievance was based upon false sentiment; before Venetian rule, civic bodies had had to work alongside the nominees of despotic rulers.

Since Venetian rule had tended to confirm the local power of those with status and wealth, the discontent of the patricians may seem both unreasonable and surprising. Had they yearned in vain to be members of the Venetian greater council? A few, as well as papal nephews, military captains and other alien dignitaries, had this honour conferred on them, but were not expected to take their seats or vote. The case of Girolamo Savorgnan, of the leading loyalist family in Friuli, who was elected to the senate in September 1509, was a rare exception, and he had been dispatched within a week on a military mission. Venetian institutions could not have worked at all had they suddenly been flooded with non-Venetian patricians; but it is doubtful whether this was what the mainland patricians wanted in any case. Those who already claimed noble ancestry may have regarded Venetian 'nobility' as not worth having at all, but prominence locally, unaccompanied by interference from anyone, was probably what they craved most; confirmation of nobility and independence at the Emperor's hands may have been their vision of what Maximilian's invasion would mean.

Such speculations do not provide a pattern of behaviour, however, and it would be a mistake to suppose that the relations of the noble and citizen patricians of the mainland with the ruling caste of Venice were hostile. Guarino, who was an active citizen of Verona as well as a scholar with many patrician pupils, wrote in 1423, 'Thank God we have such governors! We are fortunate in having such magistrates!' Two years later, reporting to a friend on rural disorders and assaults upon officials near Verona, he exclaimed with dismay, 'that this should take place in the Venetian empire!' – as if the latter normally provided the soundest civil peace in the entire world. Similarly, it would be a mistake to suppose that Venetian patricians necessarily despised those of status in provincial society as their inferiors. In December 1509 four Paduan patricians were publicly executed outside the doge's palace for collaborating with Leonardo Trissino of Vicenza, the Emperor's ennobled puppet ruler, during his short occupation of their city. Since the surrender in June had been on Venetian orders, Luigi da Porto not only presented this as a travesty of justice, but suggested there was widespread sympathy for the condemned men among friends in Venetian high society, where he too moved with ease.

An infinite variety of individual calculations lie behind the treasons and loyalties to Venice in the League of Cambrai war.

55 'The Basilica': Palladio's reconstructed exterior of the Palazzo della Ragione, or council hall, Vicenza (commissioned in 1549).

56 Palazzo Chiericati, Vicenza: an urban villa commissioned from Palladio by a local patrician in 1551.

The most conspicuous traitor, Leonardo Trissino, had previously been banned from Venetian territory for committing a murder, and so he had nothing to lose. Others found the decision more difficult. The Trento family of Verona was divided, two brothers supporting the Emperor and two others supporting Venice, so that whatever happened they hoped to preserve some of the family property. The da Porto of Vicenza were neutral or cautiously pro-Trissino in the beginning, but reverted to Venice when they had been disillusioned, first by Maximilian's delay in arriving, then by Trissino's presumption and finally by the arrogance and brutality of the Germans. The defection in September 1511 of Antonio Savorgnan, whose dynasty had been the ultra-loyalists in Friuli, a bulwark against many of the rural gentry who resented Venetian protection of the peasantry, can be best explained by family rivalry and concern for his own person. His enemies in Venice grudged his great authority in the region, and he was suspected of exploiting a riot at Udine for his own advantage; clearly there was a better prospect for him on Maximilian's side.

Many of those who hovered to see which way the wind would blow, or who in 1509 submitted to the enemy, can hardly have done so out of a long-standing grievance against Venice; their immediate concern was self-preservation and fear of all they had being ravaged. After the defeat at Agnadello (1509), the citizens of Brescia closed their gates to the retreating Venetian army, but this was from fear of becoming the victims of a siege and sack by the victorious French. At Treviso, while some of the patricians were in favour of submitting to Trissino in June 1509, their calculation of advantage changed rapidly with events. They realized Trissino had no army; they were afraid when the lesser citizens, craftsmen and shopkeepers shouted for St Mark, and convinced when the threat came from Venice that the city would be sacked if it defected. 'Pacific and quiet people', was the official report of the *podestà* and captain of Treviso in 1563, and throughout the surrounding countryside, 'all are truly heartfelt in their devotion to the name of St Mark'. Such, under normal conditions, was the prevailing impression: too many inferences should not be drawn from the panic of 1509.

The just order of society, to those who governed the Venetian empire, was the traditional patrician order in every locality since this, if loyal, was the best guarantee of peace and Venetian business. Contempt for any other elements, though not the proclaimed policy of the republic, was clearly the usual attitude: the governor (*luogotenente*) of Udine in August 1509, Antonio Giustinian, made no bones about his opinion of the city's unusually 'open' council. 'Cobblers, smiths and tailors should attend to their own business and not meddle in government', he declared. The revolt of Antonio Savorgnan provided an occasion to remodel the government of Udine after 1513.

Yet the Venetian government was cautious when it was faced by protest or revolt against local patricians, lest this should turn into rebellion against Venice itself. On the mainland this scarcely occurred; known rebels were severely treated, but a policy of reconciliation was followed, in, for instance, Verona, Padua and Brescia immediately after the League of Cambrai war had ended in 1516. Overseas it was more serious. Popular rebellions had broken out in almost every locality of Dalmatia and Albania from 1507 onwards. Official policy was to pacify without repression, but the officers sent to do the pacifying acted in the light of their own prejudices, regarding any protest against the existing order as a rebellion against Venice. Sebastiano Giustinian took the toughest line possible in his punitive expedition during the summer of 1512. Having dealt with Zara, he told the citizens of Sebenico that he had come to liberate those 'who had been compelled to live under the tyranny of humble citizens'; the freedom of the city and its free magistrates were to be restored. There and in the island of Lesina (Hvar) he made havoc, treating the rebels against their own incompetent and idle patricians as terrorist outlaws. It is not surprising that Giustinian was recalled before he could finish the job. When troubles broke out again on Lesina in 1514, Vincenzo Cappello also interpreted his commission with the utmost ruthlessness. Yet his orders had been ambiguous: 'Proceed against the culprits with whatever severe censure is in keeping with justice and the dignity of our state, bearing in mind always the security of our interests.' Cautious pragmatism: it would be hard to find a better summary of the spirit of Venetian justice and public relations than these instructions.

57, 58 Doge Ziani with pope Alexander III and the Emperor Frederick Barbarossa (1177): a cherished occasion in Venetian history. Above, the doge is presented with a ceremonial sunshade or umbrella; below, the doge stands between pope and Emperor.

IV VENETIAN CIVILIZATION

The problem of what to select in trying to portray a 'civiliza-tion' is, as Jacob Burkhardt confessed, almost insoluble; one cannot display more than a few fragments, depending on personal choice. Some of the qualities which contemporaries held to be typical of Venetian life have already been discussed: the established forms of government and society, the pursuit of mercantile profit, the pride in justice, and the mystique of a state adorned with some of the fashions of neo-Roman human-ism. Yet civilization embraces the whole environment, spiritual and physical. What forms did religion take in the city of St Mark? What were the material and moral conditions of life in the metropolis of the Venetian empire? What were the special Venetian contributions to learning, literature and art? These are vast subjects, but something must be said about them all.

THE BOSOM OF CHRISTIANITY

'The Venetians must be greatly aided by God in their affairs because they are very solicitous about divine worship,' the Milanese canon Casola wrote in 1494, commenting, as other observers did, upon the solemnity and discipline of their services, as well as the number of splendid churches in the city. His remark may be a pious *non sequitur*, but at least it emphasizes that religion made a strong contribution to the cohesion of Venetian society and the régime.

Secular and ecclesiastical went closely together in Venice. The heads of the lay hierarchy, the doge and procurators of St Mark's, were almost sacred dignitaries, and the doge spent much of his time at religious functions. The wall-paintings commissioned for the hall of the greater council referred to the pope's visit and the great reconciliation of 1177; Guariento's vast painting above the Tribune represented Paradise. Outside the doge's palace, sculptures of the late fourteenth and the

59, 60 Scriptural reminders of human frailty on the outside of the doge's palace
(c. 1400): the Drunkenness of Noah and the Temptation of Adam and Eve.

fifteenth century taught theological as well as civil doctrine. On
the façade facing the waterfront were the Archangel Michael
with the Temptation of Adam and Eve at one corner, and the
Archangel Raphael with the Drunkenness of Noah (illustrating
man's depravity after the Fall) at the other. Inside the courtyard,
the ornamental 'Foscari Arch' bore in its niches Antonio Rizzo's
marble Adam and Eve, but also the statue of a shield-bearer
thought to be Mars, besides numerous pseudo-Roman worthies
and warriors on its pinnacles. How much the cult of St Mark
pervaded Venetian life has already been stressed. Four separate
festivals were dedicated to him alone, and the reminders of his
protective presence were legion.

61 A strangely assorted company of figures above the 'Foscari Arch' ▶

It occurred to Pius II, writing one of the furious passages of his memoirs, that the Venetian state was less inspired by religion than Venetian religion was identified with the state.

They wish to appear Christians before the world, but in reality they never think of God and, except for the state, which they regard as a deity, they hold nothing sacred, nothing holy. To a Venetian that is just which is for the good of the state; that is pious which increases the empire. . . . What the senate approves is holy even though it is opposed to the Gospel.

This was rather less than fair. Certainly a great number of political expedients and opportunist policies were justified in the name of religion and the interests of St Mark. 'We live in peace because God is peace', doge Mocenigo declared in 1423, 'and whoever wants war may go to hell.' He might have said, more justly, that Venetians preferred peace because peace was good for trade, but when their interests demanded it, they went to war as ardently as anyone else. On the other hand, there was nothing spurious about the faith in Venice as a holy city; 'the bosom of Christianity', Marin Sanudo even called it in the preface to his description of Venetian institutions, *Cronachetta* (1493). Such faith was expressed in both imperialistic and devotional ways.

Patrician families took pride in their service to Christendom not only through Church endowments and the duties they performed for St Mark, but also on account of their many sons and daughters who were professionals in religion. The number of Venetian prelates of the Church in the fifteenth and sixteenth centuries is out of all proportion to those from the patriciates of other cities. The Venetian empire afforded them an extra-ordinary number of dignities: three patriarchates (Aquileia, Constantinople and Venice-Grado), five archbishoprics and thirty-eight bishoprics, to say nothing of the office of *primicerio* (arch-priest) of St Mark's, abbacies, canonries and numerous other benefices. The patriarch of Venice (the title was trans-ferred from Grado to the former bishopric of Venice in 1451) was invariably a cleric of patrician family, as was the patriarch of Aquileia after 1470; the titular patriarch of Constantinople, whose seat had been transferred to Negroponte, was more often than not a Venetian. Nominations to major benefices were made by the senate, and approval in the court of Rome was often a mere formality, while appointments to the parish churches of Venice were decided locally, by election among property-owners.

Nor was this ecclesiastical empire confined to the Venetian regions of Christendom. It extended to Rome as well during this period. In 1406, for the first time in history, a Venetian patrician was elected pope in the person of Angelo Correr (Gregory XII). This was at an unfortunate time, and Gregory's diffidence about ending the schism in the western Church was such that the Venetian government (which had tried to remain neutral) even withdrew obedience when the council of Pisa, called by rebel cardinals of both obediences, elected a third pope in 1409. Nevertheless, this pope, too, was a subject of the Venetian empire: Pietro Filargi of Crete (Alexander V). The honours were continued with the election of Gregory XII's nephew, Gabriele Condulmer, as pope Eugenius IV (1431–47) who, as befitted the citizen of a Greco-Latin empire, presided over the attempted reunion of Catholic and Orthodox Churches in 1439; and again with Pietro Barbo's election as Paul II (1464–71). Over thirty Venetian patricians were members of the college of cardinals in the fifteenth and sixteenth centuries, and several of them narrowly missed becoming pope; Paul II's nephew, Marco Barbo, and Domenico Grimani, a principal spokesman for Venetian interests at the papal court in the early sixteenth century, were tipped as the favourites in different conclaves. Clerical careers and ambitions for the apostolic headship of the Church were of course more the individual's concern than the government's; by laws of the late fifteenth century patricians holding Church benefices were not allowed to sit in the greater council, or hold secular office; exceptions may have been allowed but on the whole the republic discouraged service to the Church. Nevertheless all these illustrious Venetian prelates bore witness to the lactescence of 'the bosom of Christianity'.

The Christian reverence of Venice was most fervently expressed in external forms. The enormous number of sacred objects, some giving occasion for elaborate processions and mass veneration, impressed both inhabitants and visitors with a sense of the city's peculiar sanctity, reminiscent of the early Crusaders' reverence for Constantinople. This was appropriate, seeing that so many of the treasures had in fact been stolen from Constantinople in 1204 and that Venice was the port from which hundreds of pilgrims set sail every year for the Holy Land; a traveller like Fra Felix Fabri, who went to Jerusalem in both

62, 63 Left, Cardinal Bessarion, Greek admirer and benefactor of Venice, in veneration beside a reliquary. Right, the relic of the Holy

1480 and 1483, was able to pass the month or more of waiting for a passage by going the rounds of Venetian shrines. Besides St Mark himself, there were supposed to be over fifty other saints' bodies in Venice, together with innumerable relics, and the collection was always increasing. The famous fragment of the True Cross had been presented to the Scuola of S. Giovanni Evangelista in 1369; St Athanasius's body arrived in 1455; St George's head was brought from Aegina in 1462; the body of St Roch (S. Rocco), an enviable talisman against the plague, was acquired about 1485.

Religious discipline was observed by thousands of the lay population as well as by those under monastic rules. Pious fraternities were to be found in all Italian cities, but there was

Cross being carried by members of the Scuola of S. Giovanni Evangelista to a funeral at S. Lio; from a painting by Giovanni Mansueti.

64 Scuola of S. Giovanni Evangelista: entrance to the courtyard designed by Pietro Lombardo (*c.* 1481).

nothing quite like the leading Venetian institutions of this sort, the *scuole grandi*. Four of them, S. Maria della Carità, the Misericordia, S. Marco, and S. Giovanni Evangelista, had originated as flagellant societies in the thirteenth century; the fraternity of S. Rocco was added to their number in 1481, and that of S. Teodoro in 1552. Their purpose was to promote virtuous living, and to distribute benefits, both material and spiritual, among their members, and to some extent among the needy outside. Rich or poor might join, at different rates of subscription, but those denounced for sinful behaviour were fined or expelled. Corporate funds were enormous, and were spent lavishly on the architecture and interior decoration of the meeting-houses. This earned them a place among the sights of Venice, though there was criticism of such spending in the sixteenth century.

65 Scuola of S. Marco: the façade designed by Mauro Coducci and the Lombardi. At ground level are lions in relief perspective guarding the doorway, and two scenes from the life of St Mark.

The *scuole grandi* were independent foundations, but the state expected them to play a part in the processions on public occasions, and to contribute money to public causes, including war. They were not governed by the patricians, although the latter kept a watchful interest over their affairs, and were closely associated as patrons. Instead, management was left to that lesser *élite*, the citizens, who modelled their administration on patrician institutions of government; for themselves there were elections to short-term offices, executive councils, and robed magnificence; for all members, there were the annual chapter meetings, which provided a rough equivalent to the greater council. It is tempting to suppose that the *scuole grandi* added significantly to the social stability and civil peace of Venice: they provided a gratifying outlet for self-important citizens, and an austere moral influence upon the population.

A different species of devotional fervour also flourished in Venice, which inspired several generations of patricians to believe they were called to regenerate Christendom. Beginning in the late fourteenth century, the spiritual movement for reform in the religious orders, and the quest for a more intro-spective, Biblical and contemplative religion (known in the north as the *devotio moderna*) took various forms in Venice. The earliest house of Observant Dominicans was founded there in 1393; and in 1404 the cousins Gabriele Condulmer and Antonio Correr founded a house for secular canons on the island of San Giorgio in Alga, rather reminiscent of the community of Windesheim in the Netherlands. Ludovico Barbo, another patrician associated with this community, entered the Bene-dictine Order and introduced a stricter observance to the monastery of S. Giustina in Padua in 1407.

It would be vain to try and trace all that followed from these endeavours, but it was in the same rather austere tradition of Venetian devoutness that the ardent papalist Domenico de' Domenichi, bishop of Torcello and Brescia, presented his radical proposals for reform of the curia to Pius II in 1458, and that two earnest patricians, Vincenzo Querini and Tommaso

66 Gasparo Contarini (1483–1542), active patrician and devout reformer, who wrote of Venice: 'No state has existed which possesses institutions and laws equally apt to lead to a good and blissful life.' He became a cardinal in 1534.

Giustinian, made theirs to pope Leo X during the Fifth Lateran Council in 1513. This pair, who had rechristened themselves Peter and Paul, respectively, had started by holding readings of scriptural and patristic works with a group of patrician laymen who met in the Giustinian family house on the island of Murano; they then joined the Benedictine community of Camaldoli, and set out to reform it. Querini and Giustinian emphasized many of the same points as others who tried to reform the Church from within: the value of internal regeneration by grace, regular preaching and translations of the Bible.

Perhaps the most intense of these patrician evangelists in the early sixteenth century was Gasparo Contarini, who had undergone a mystical experience not unlike Luther's during Holy Week of 1511, convincing him of the immediate efficacy of divine grace as a means of salvation. Best known for his eulogistic writings upon the government of Venice, Contarini also wrote a treatise on the ideal bishop, for whom he took as his model another devout patrician, Pietro Barozzi, bishop of Padua from 1487 to 1507. Contarini's influence was profound upon many zealous ecclesiastics, including Pietro Lipomanno, for whom, as bishop-elect of Bergamo, the treatise had been written, and Gianmatteo Giberti (bishop of Verona 1524–44).

Personifying not only the new piety, but going back to the position of doge Ziani in 1177 as Venetian mediator of Christendom, Contarini tried in vain to arrange a compromise between the Catholic Church and the Lutherans at the Diet of Ratisbon (1541).

The difference between this sort of religious zeal and Protestant zeal was not, as Contarini realized, very great; all the less in a city which, while fervent in devotion to the saints and other external forms of religion, preserved so much independence from the papacy. The pretensions of Venice as a peculiarly holy city had not, of course, allowed any tolerance of heresy; the government of St Mark had reserved this offence to secular jurisdiction since the thirteenth century, and there was no abandonment now of its professed orthodoxy; in 1541 a new magistracy of thirteen sages (*savi*) was instituted with special competence for heresy trials. Even so, there seems to have been a certain expectation that Venice would be the source for Italy of a reconciliation and reform of the Church. In December 1542, Bernardo Ochino wrote from his exile in Geneva to an unknown Venetian patrician:

God knows how much I want to see Christ reign in my Venice, for it to be free of every diabolical yoke. . . . Already Christ has begun to penetrate in Italy, but I would like Him to enter glorious from the start, and I believe Venice will be the door. What happiness to you if you accept Him, and woe to those who with Herod persecute Him out of human fear.

An anonymous letter to doge Francesco Donà, after his election in November 1545, alluded to the Contarini-like views he was supposed to hold, congratulating him on the benefits he would be able to confer not only on Venice but the whole of Christianity. 'If the clemency of God does not avail itself of so rare a medium as Your Serenity and not help us to reform . . . surely we will no longer know where to turn.'

Many Protestant or semi-Protestant academies of patricians continued to flourish, and so did artisan conventicles; since so many German merchants in Venice were Lutherans, the practicability and advantages of persecution would seem all the more doubtful. As Cristoforo da Canale wrote in his *Della Milizia marittima*, not only true but also false religions have their usefulness for peace; and the blind eye was the best way of proclaiming this. Papal nuncios were able to exert a certain pressure, and by the 1560s condemnation of those irretrievably 'lost' was becoming more common in Venice. Even so, as late as 1580, Giacomo Broccardo, a parish priest in Venice who had tutored a number of distinguished patricians in unorthodoxy, prophesied in his writings that two councils of the Protestant faith would be held in Venice, making it the capital of a reformed Christendom in place of Rome: an imaginative variation on the theme of Venetian-Roman parity or superiority.

Whatever Pius II may have thought, religion was a powerful bond in Venetian civilization; perhaps even more binding than the other neo-Roman bonds of law and duty, for it took on a greater variety of forms, and expressed far more than the self-preserving instincts of the ruling caste. Patricians no doubt differed widely in the ways they understood or practised Christianity; Marin Sanudo, for instance, expressed more devout sentiments in his diary than did the gossiping Girolamo Priuli. For Sanudo, as for Gasparo Contarini or Daniele Barbaro, the politically active and learned patrician who became patriarch of Aquileia in 1550, religion had an exalted and special relevance to Venetian government and society.

Daniele Barbaro's philosophy of the Venetian state is expressed in Paolo Paruta's dialogue, *On the Perfection of the Political Life*, written in 1579 but professing to be the record of a discussion between various lay and clerical patricians in 1563. Barbaro is given the last word, and exclaims in the manner of a prophet:

The city must abound in temples and priests, and holy ceremonies be performed with the utmost magnificence, so that these external things may excite internal emotion and bear witness to it. Meanwhile, the piety of the Prince, as it were a clear light burning, should awaken in

67 Daniele Barbaro (1514–70), like Contarini a devout practitioner of the active life: a distinguished Aristotelian scholar, editor of Vitruvius, and writer on eloquence and aesthetic theory.

the hearts of all the love of goodness; this alone can form the perfect civil life which, together with fear of the laws, one seeks to introduce in the world.

METROPOLITAN LIFE

The *Dominante*, or seat of the Venetian republic and first city of the empire, was small by comparison with ancient Rome, but vast by comparison with most other European cities during the fifteenth and sixteenth centuries. The engraved view of

Venice in 1500 gives a description of this urban sprawl upon the lagoon which words cannot achieve; nor can the life within it be anatomized in a few pages.

It was a crowded city. The exact size of the population during the fifteenth century cannot be reckoned; Marin Sanudo declared in 1493 that it was 150,000 according to recent calculations, though a figure nearer to 100,000 would probably be the century's average, allowing for the periodic reductions by mass disease; 115,000 is the total more reliably estimated for 1509. The biggest rise in population seems to have occurred during the relatively healthy middle decades of the sixteenth century, so that by 1563, when a fairly comprehensive census system was used, nearly 170,000 people were recorded as resident in the metropolis. Counting of heads in Venice was complicated by the temporary absence of so many inhabitants, from ships' crews to administrators, and the temporary presence at certain times of an inflated population of foreign merchants, pilgrims and other visitors, as well as refugees, who came for either political or economic reasons, from both overseas and mainland. Such movement of people gave Venice not only the character of a great Mediterranean port, but the flavour of a cosmopolitan capital as well. 'The metropolis of all Italy' was the hyperbolic description Francesco Sansovino used (quoting his father) in the classic Venetian guide-book he published in 1581, *Venetia città nobilissima et singolare*.

In consequence, it was a cramped city. During the late 1450s senate resolutions calling for a new property valuation emphasized the continuous building upon both new and old sites, and the soaring rents. Marin Sanudo gave an example of this in 1493 from the profits his own family made as landlords, charging 800 ducats a year just for a tavern and a few shops near the new fish market; at this rate, the rents collected by Venice's biggest property-owners, religious foundations, the *scuole grandi* and the procurators' trust of St Mark, must have been enormous. The map of 1500 illustrates the mass and density of building which by then had covered all the city's original island parishes.

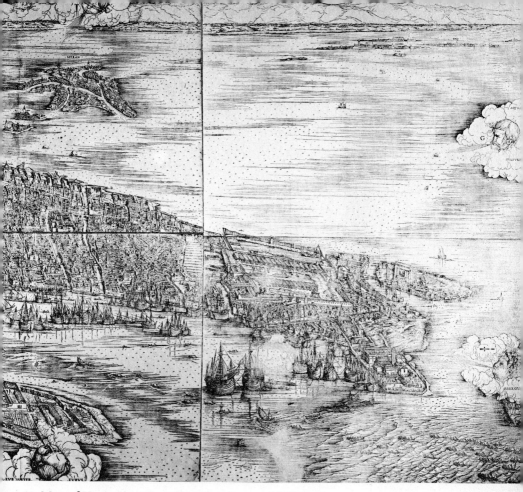

68 Map of Venice (1500) attributed to Jacopo de' Barbari.

This pressure upon living space seems to have had some social effects which were paradoxical in such a caste-dominated city. The patrician families, so small a proportion of the total population, did not dominate neighbourhoods as they dominated government. The richest and most status-conscious built upon narrow frontages along the Grand Canal, but even these were known as houses rather than palaces, and could afford little exterior effect beyond a pretentious façade; nor could they all be near the most sought-after and expensive sites in the capital,

125

◄ 69 Rialto, the commercial centre of Venice. Detail from Jacopo de' Barbari's map (above).

the government and business districts of St Mark's and the Rialto Bridge. Many of the patricians could not emulate the Loredan, the Cornaro or the Grimani, with their pompous new canal houses faced with Istrian stone, which adapted the Roman orders of architecture to a Venetian setting in the late fifteenth and early sixteenth centuries. They had to distribute themselves throughout the city in rented as well as owner-occupied buildings; they often moved house (leases under Venetian law could not be for longer than five years) and large dynastic groups did not congregate within a single street or parish. Some families lived in the poorer districts of Castello, containing the Arsenal, or Santa Croce, which included the fishermen's quarter of San Nicolò.

The accommodation problem also meant that household establishments had to be small, quite apart from any mean dislike of spending. In 1494 canon Casola found the patricians 'frugal and very modest in their manner of living at home'. Nearly a century later, Montaigne made the same comment and Coryate, early in the seventeenth century, was astonished to see senators doing their own shopping in the markets. Since movement about the city had to be on foot, or in a narrow boat upon canals jammed with traffic, the patrician was far more exposed than he would have been, aloof upon horseback, on

126

73 View looking up the Grand Canal, from above the Rialto Bridge. The Palazzo dei Camerlenghi is shown on the left, and a corner is just visible (right) of the warehouse (*fondaco*) of the German merchants ▶

70, 71, 72 Three patrician palaces displaying neo-Roman architectural motifs; left to right: Palazzo Dario (*c.* 1480), Palazzo Cornaro-Spinelli (end of the fifteenth century), Palazzo Loredan, now Vendramin-Calergi (early sixteenth century).

the mainland. On a *barchetta* or *gondola*, which Marin Sanudo reckoned was more expensive to keep than a horse and groom, patricians might display their rank by having two men to row them instead of the usual one, but it was hardly an exclusive craft: in 1581, Francesco Sansovino estimated, there were between 9000 and 10,000 of them.

If not social levelling, perhaps some sort of social leavening occurred in these conditions, and contributed to the lack of conflict between the classes of Venetian society. Nevertheless, housing in a city of such high rents must have been appalling for the greater number of inhabitants, and if the very rich were only a few, an enormous gulf remained between the moderately well-off patricians and citizens and the ordinary working populace. Sanudo's remark that everyone in Venice lived like lords in the late fifteenth century seems as complacent an exaggeration as Priuli's that everyone by then had a little place in the country. Of the aristocracy among manual workers, the *arsenalotti*, who were at least as numerous as the aristocracy of the greater council, even a master shipwright is reckoned to have earned no more than 50 ducats a year. Precious little is known about such people, but less skilled labourers, such as galley oarsmen, dockers, boatmen and porters, must have been much poorer.

Compared to other cities, however, there is no doubt that there was high employment in Venice, and except during times of unusual scarcity and war, there are no descriptions of crowds of starving beggars. Bread, and fresh fruit and vegetables ferried from market gardens on the lagoon islands, were plentiful and cheap; all travellers' descriptions insist on this point. Prices were controlled in the consumer's interest by the officials of the *justitia vecchia*, who also inspected weights and measures. Sometimes there were distributions of free corn: understandably, the death of Pius II in 1464 was an occasion for such state bounty and 400 bushels were given to the poor. The want of fresh water from springs and fountains added to the difficulties of domestic life, but to some extent the need

74 Well-head (*vero da pozzo*) above a rainwater cistern; fifteenth century.

was met by numerous rainwater cisterns and a regular service of barges bringing water from the river Brenta.

There was more public concern for hygiene in Venice than in many cities which were built on hills and enjoyed running water. Foul smells were common enough; Pero Tafur, a Spanish visitor, described in 1438 the attempt to smother them by burning aromatic spices in the streets; and needless to say Pius II sneered at Venice for its stinks (he thought Strasbourg superior as a town because it was less smelly). Nevertheless, a magistracy paid from rates levied on property had been responsible for the clearance and dredging of the canals and disposal of rubbish since the thirteenth century. Perhaps it was neglectful, and certainly the increasing population must have made the problem more acute. In 1485 a board of public health was instituted (*provveditori alla sanità*), with special authority over street cleaning, cisterns, vagabonds, prostitutes, burials and other matters. In February 1493, the senate approved a proposal that the government should provide twelve barges each with one or two men to collect filth and rubbish; in 1558 permanent jobs were created for cleaners of each ward or *sestiere*, who were responsible for seeing that the whole city was cleaned up four times a month.

Venice was a dangerous city. The crime rate was high, for all the boasted concord and lack of organized rebellion. Private acts of violence were common, and easily committed in the setting of narrow, dark alleyways, shadowy piazzas and canals. The statutes of the *signori di notte*, the special night magistracy which patrolled the streets of the six districts, illustrate the concern with this familiar problem of the Italian cities, though it may be questioned how effective the *signori* were, or could be. In 1408, for instance, it was ordained that the offence of being found with a sharp knife, whether large or small, should carry a 20 lire fine and fifteen days imprisonment. There is a surviving register of the *signori di notte* from 1472 to 1507 which lists the details of many violent crimes resulting in death, patricians as well as others being involved; wounding which was not mortal and so unrecorded was presumably many times more frequent. In his youth, Pietro Bembo (1470–1547) had a finger cut off in a quarrel. The sordid violence beneath the smooth surface of Venetian life is illustrated at its most macabre in 1503, when a man was condemned to death for selling cooked meat which was identified as human flesh.

Nor was private violence quite without expression in political life. No doge was assassinated during this period, but there were some attempts on their lives, such as Andrea Contarini's plan to murder doge Foscari in 1426. On a November night in 1450, Almoro Donà, the acting head of the council of ten, was quietly urinating in a doorway on Campo Santa Maria Formosa when he was stabbed from behind; he died two days later from the unidentified assault. Violence could even erupt in the greater council, as it did when Domenico Calbo struck Benedetto Minotto in the eye in 1498, for which act of contempt he was exiled to Cyprus.

Civility in the more liberal and compassionate sense of the word was not perhaps an outstanding quality of this perilous city; the less fortunate and least privileged suffered. In this

Venice was not exceptional, and like other cities it had a large number of charitable foundations which tried to relieve distress from the standpoint of Christian philanthropy: Marin Sanudo lists over thirty different hospitals in Venice, though it is not clear what kind of treatment could be obtained in them. Corporations tended to look after their own poor and sick, though among the *scuole grandi* the Misericordia had a special concern for the welfare of prisoners, as the Scuola of S. Rocco had for plague sufferers. The *arsenalotti* had their own welfare benefits; until 1440 one out of every six shipwrights had to be over fifty-five, so that nominal work was available for the older and less able-bodied; after this date a tax within their craft guild provided a pension fund. In the same way as the craft guilds, the patricians also looked after their poor; the provision of sinecure posts has already been mentioned, but there were special bequests for the relief of poor patricians and cheap tenements reserved for them by private benefactors.

Welfare provided by the government was, however, rather thin: even in the case of impoverished patricians, a proposal in 1492 that 70,000 ducats should be spent on their relief was rejected, and its promoters were punished. The state's action during plague epidemics, banishment to the deadly *lazaretti* or boarding up of the victims inside their own houses, expressed little human feeling beyond the desperate instinct of self-preservation; and a callous fatalism towards human misery was displayed in the winter of 1527–28 when famine, flood and war on the mainland brought crowds of desperate refugees into Venice, and children were left to die in the streets. However, a more positive social paternalism was gaining ground at this time; in the following winter various measures were taken, including a ban on begging (non-Venetian beggars were sent back where they had come from) and a special property rate levied to relieve distress. This rate paid for emergency hospitals to cope with epidemics of typhus and plague, assistance to sick families boarded up in their own homes and attempts to find work for the able-bodied.

These grave measures taken in 1528–29 seem to acknowledge at least some ethic of human dignity; so, at about the same time, did Girolamo Emiliani's Congregation of Somasca (near Bergamo) for the teaching of orphans, and San Gaetano Thiene's hospital for the incurables. But in general the Venetians' professed love of liberty should not be understood in terms of the liberty of the individual human being. This is illustrated by their attitude to slavery. So long as slaves were available, the Venetians had traded in them, and doge Mocenigo, in his speech of 1423, declared that 50,000 ducats had been collected by the import and re-export taxes upon slaves since 1414. The supply decreased as the Turks came to dominate so many of the sources, but household slaves still existed at the end of the fifteenth century, as the decorative Negro gondoliers in Carpaccio's paintings illustrate, and there was plantation serfdom in Crete and Cyprus. The Venetian economy did not depend upon slavery (the galleys were rowed by paid *galleotti* and after 1540 by prisoners, never by slaves) but there is little evidence of moral objection to its indignity. A motion debated by the senate in August 1459 was mildly humane but not abolitionist in tone: it deplored the re-export of so many slaves brought into Venice, and, 'considering the penury and hardship of so many of the slaves of our gentlemen and citizens', proposed that slave traders should register exactly the number and quality of the slaves they were shipping before they entered the port. Perhaps the Venetians failed to be new Romans in terms of depending on slave labour only because the human heads were not available.

Most foreign minorities who settled in Venice to pursue their own interests, Germans, Slavs and Greeks, for instance, seem to have been tolerated or even assimilated at all levels of society. The presence of so many non-Venetians, including mainlanders, among the working population of the city, remarked upon by Fra Felix Fabri, may help to explain the plebeian peace: many came only to find work (opportunities were great as mortality was so high) and established no roots

75 Arrival of *podestà*
Sebastiano Contarini
in Capo d'Istria, 1517.

in the place. One would expect, however, to find conflict and prejudice between one racial or provincial group and another, and suspicion of Greeks in particular. Giovanni Bembo, writing about his deceased Corfiote wife in 1536, remarked with satisfaction that, although she was Greek, she did not like Greeks herself.

But common humanity failed, as in other cities, when it came to the Jews. This was not entirely racial prejudice, for Jews who practised as doctors in the city were not persecuted with the rest; it was as money-lenders and pawnbrokers that they were most resented, as an alien religious community which exploited Christian resources for its own superficially unproductive ends. That this was unreasonable resentment was sometimes admitted; during periods of war or post-war financial strain, the government's own interest was served by toleration, since the Jews' money enabled taxpayers to raise small loans and thus meet their obligations, as well as providing the republic with additional revenue from the tribute Jews were made to pay.

133

But prejudice and persecution were more often found; partly, perhaps, because the Jews often took religious objects in pawn. Since the early fourteenth century, there had been attempts to restrict Jews to the mainland, and a law, ridiculous because it was so easily evaded, forbade them to visit the city for longer than two weeks at a time. By the end of the century they were required to wear yellow badges, and by a law of 1423 forbidden to own real property. Prejudice rose and fell; it reached a hysterical level during the height of Fra Bernardino of Feltre's influence in the 1470s, and again towards the end of the League of Cambrai war, possibly owing to the great increase of immigration to the city, and, since so many private banks collapsed in the period 1494–1520, the difficulty of raising money from other sources. In 1516, the *ghetto* was instituted, a segregated compound for Jews, patrolled and locked at night; they were obliged to pay an annual tribute of 6000 ducats to the

76 Left, Ponte San Lorenzo, painted by Gentile Bellini, with members of the Scuola of S. Giovanni Evangelista watching their *Guardiano* swimming to recover the relic of the True Cross (a celebrated episode of the past).

77 The Rialto Bridge, depicted by Carpaccio. Congestion was a social problem in Venice, but it may have helped to make class barriers less oppressive.

government. Marin Sanudo noted in his diary a senate debate in November 1519 which revealed some extreme views: those of Gabriel Moro, for instance, who even alleged that the duke of Milan (Ludovico Sforza) had lost his state in 1499 on account of the favour he had shown the Jews. Sanudo himself reflected more moderately, 'If I had been in the senate as in times past, I would have spoken, not for the Jews so much as for the necessity to have them; pawnbrokers are needed in a country for the benefit of all.'

Women hardly come into the category of those oppressed by inhumanity and lack of privilege, but this half of the city's population may be considered, too, as at least the dupes of Venetian pride and hypocrisy. In art, the republic was often personified as a woman, a voluptuous sea-born Venus-Venice, and in Titian's paintings particularly, the female nude acquired a heroic grandeur equal to the idealized male nudes of Florentine artists. This was no sign of indulgence to female power. Venice was the bridegroom, not the bride or daughter of the sea, when the doge performed the ancient ritual of casting a ring overboard the state barge every Ascension Day. The doge's wife, or *dogaressa*, was a mere consort without authority; usually an old woman, she did not even have much power of social attraction.

Patrician privileges descended only through the male line, and for many girls the prospect of life must have been bleak indeed. The earliest book printed in Italy, according to some scholars, was the manual on bringing up girls, the *Decor Puellarum* dated at Venice, 1461. Patrician and citizen daughters passed from childhood decorum to the secluded conventions of marriage laid down in Francesco Barbaro's unctuous *De Re Uxoria* (1415); if their parents could not muster a sufficient dowry, either from family or charitable funds, the most lively future was as a nun or a prostitute. Perhaps Venetian women enjoyed secret influence through the confidences of their husbands and lovers, but the scope was probably limited in such a poker-faced society. The younger and more concupiscent women compensated with their notorious dressiness, breast

78 An unknown Venetian woman painted by Palma il Vecchio.

79 Dogaressa Giovanna (*née* Dandolo), wife of doge Pasquale Malipiero (1457–62). In her widowhood this remarkable dogaressa became a patroness of the new art of printing.

display, false hair, make-up and jewellery, which no male-enacted sumptuary laws seem to have been able to prevent; while the others, wearing black, endured their lives in morbid boredom. Working women were also at a disadvantage. Women sailmakers in the Arsenal might earn 12 ducats a year (less than a novice shipwright) while their male overseer received over three times as much.

It was hard for a woman with artistic or intellectual talent to express herself. Tintoretto's daughter, Marietta, was quite a skilful painter, but her father (classified as a citizen) is said to have paid her the double insult of making her dress like a boy, and then forbidding her to leave home and make her own career, in spite of pressing invitations from foreign courts. A few exceptional women managed to distinguish themselves, but these emphasize the usual state of exclusion. Isotta Nogarola of Verona, a provincial bluestocking with some literary talent, complained to Guarino in 1436 that she was often sorry she

137

80 Housebound Venetian women: detail from Giovanni Mansueti's painting of the procession outside S. Lio.

81 Left, Venetian novice taking the veil of a religious order, from a convent service book (1523).
82 Above, Veronica Franco.

had been born a woman, since the whole town sneered at her
and described her as an obelisk of brazenness; Guarino rightly
reproved her for such self-betrayal of female sensitivity, but he
acknowledged that in antiquity she would have been immor-
talized. Several women of citizen descent made their mark in
Venice as high-class courtesans, capable of composing Latin
orations and presiding over literary *salons*; such were Gaspara
Stampa, Veronica Franco and Cassandra Fedele, a poetess who
corresponded with Poliziano and died in 1556 at the age of 102.
Mention should also be made of Caterina Cornaro, the ex-
queen of Cyprus, who was presented with Asolo (near Treviso)
as a private fief in her retirement, and had the distinction of
being the only female ruler on Venetian territory. Her court
was celebrated, probably with flattering inaccuracy, in a literary
dialogue by Pietro Bembo, but in fact there seems to be

83 Portrait of a woman by Giovanni Bellini (1515), with a *terraferma*
background.

no evidence that she was an intellectual luminary. Cassandra Fedele and Caterina Cornaro were each honoured by the title 'Daughter of the Republic', exceptional but rather meaningless male amends, which might on careful consideration be taken as no less disrespectful to St Mark than Pietro Aretino's description of Venice as 'a female pope among cities' was to St Peter.

In some ways squalid and inhumane, Venice was still the most written-about city in Europe, with the possible exception of Rome itself. Its striking site and aspect were a much repeated theme, though the resemblances between Venice and Rome in these respects were rather slight. Venice had no hills, no rational road system and no gates; it was built upon open sewers instead of underground drains; not only did it have no aqueducts and hence no fountains, no horses and hence no hippodrome, but it could boast no amphitheatres, public baths, nor triumphal arches (unless one counts the cramped, top-heavily decorated 'Foscari Arch' in the palace courtyard). Venetian doges, dis-

84 Opposite, Erasmo da
Narni ('Gattamelata'),
designed and executed by
Donatello between 1446 and
1450 and erected outside the
basilica of St Antony, Padua.

85 Bartolomeo Colleoni,
designed by Verrocchio
between 1479 and 1488,
completed by Alessandro
Leopardi.

tinguished statesmen, and heroes of war (such as Carlo Zeno
of the war of Chioggia, Jacopo Marcello, victim at Gallipoli,
or Vettor Cappello of the Turkish war of 1499) were com-
memorated not by public monuments but only by tombs
erected at their families' expense. Francesco Barbaro complained to Guarino in 1421 that it had not been possible to erect
some memorial to Giorgio Loredan, who had been killed in
action at sea; celebrating individual rather than collective
achievements seems to have been deliberately discouraged by
the régime.

Even when, exceptionally, the sculptured figures of two
doges were permitted on the outer walls of the palace, Francesco Foscari on the Porta della Carta, and Andrea Gritti on
the waterfront wall, both were shown kneeling in abject
humility before the lion of St Mark. The most famous exceptions of all, two free-standing bronze statues of military
captains on horseback, were paid for from their own private 141

fortunes. Literary evidence suggests that Donatello's Erasmo da Narni ('Gattamelata') at Padua may have been formally sponsored by the senate, but on the assumption that it would be a modest figure for a tomb monument, not a triumphant caesar, and certainly not as an expense borne by the public revenues. Verrocchio's statue of Bartolomeo Colleoni could hardly have been forbidden, since he had bequeathed most of his riches to the republic, but his wish that it should stand in the Piazza San Marco was disregarded; it was banished to a much less prominent site beside the Dominican church of S. Giovanni e Paolo, faces being saved, perhaps, by the fact that this site was opposite the Scuola of S. Marco.

Ecclesiastical buildings, above all the basilica and campanile of St Mark's, the *scuole grandi*, and private patrician houses did most to create the effect of a fantastic city rising from the sea. Government building was for long rather modest. Its most imposing contribution, the doge's palace, had been begun in its present form in the 1340s, but its progress was amazingly slow.

86 The *loggetta*, a meeting-place for patricians, at the base of the campanile of St Mark's, designed by Jacopo Sansovino, *c.* 1537–49 (see pp. 184–5).

142

87 The Mint (*zecca*) designed by Sansovino.

Moreover, its name conceals the fact that, besides the apartments and council chamber of the doge, it had to contain all the other assembly halls, court rooms and offices of government, including the state prisons. Its accommodation was obviously quite inadequate, and many magistracies had to be discharged from makeshift benches in the porticoes of the palace or near the Rialto Bridge. Canon Casola commented in 1494 upon the loss of an opportunity to build much larger extensions to the palace; it seems that the patricians, some of whom complained in 1515 that far too much money had been spent uselessly on painters commissioned to decorate the hall of the greater council, were distinctly unwilling to authorize spending even for functional purposes. In the sixteenth century, however, the imperial capital did at last begin to acquire some more imposing public buildings. The new administrative block near the Rialto Bridge, the clock tower and the lodgings for the procurators on the north side of the Piazza San Marco, marked the beginning; but the zenith came with Jacopo Sansovino's neo-Vitruvian

143

architecture, the new building for the mint, all of iron and stone to reduce the fire risk, the *loggetta* at the foot of the campanile, and the splendid library and museum of antiquities. Even then, Sansovino had needed first to convince the procurators of St Mark's that his improvements to the central district of the city would increase the value of their property and rents before he received this enlightened patronage.

It may be that the average Venetian cared less about the appearance of his surroundings than the average visitor to Venice. The impression some travellers give of Venetian patricians and citizens, these new Romans, is of a decidedly sombre people. As portraits record, both classes wore a uniform garment they called a toga; it was not a white toga as in ancient Rome, but a funereal-looking black gown; in cold weather this garment was thickened with fur trimmings, and tight-fitting black caps were worn on the head. Considering that there was also a great number of clergy, both secular and regular, in Venice, and that black was the colour most of the women wore, the general effect must have been like a Swiss Sunday; canon Casola declared he felt he had arrived in a city full of doctors of law, widows and Benedictine nuns. Francesco Sansovino made similar observations in his guide-book nearly a century later: he suggested it was because the Venetians professed to be men of peace and religion that they wore such religious clothes. Admittedly, there were some variations. Members of the council of ten wore peculiarly long sleeves to their gowns, and their citizen secretaries were robed in blue or violet (variable according to the quality of the dye); senators and procurators of St Mark wore red gowns (again, of variable hues); the doge himself wore gold and white. Dress on saints' days, during mourning, or on other special occasions might show differences. Young men (including young patricians not yet eligible for the greater council, and private servants) dressed garishly; but Carpaccio's descriptive paintings show that even a private gondolier might be clothed in the standard combination of red and black.

Disciplined austerity in the social life of Venice was not only expressed by clothes. In contrast to all the madrigal singing, patrician banquets, exotic prostitutes and public spectacles, were the puritanical rules of life of the *scuole grandi*, with their rigid condemnation of blasphemy, adultery, wrath, gambling, frequenting taverns and lewd company; the moral prosecutions of the council of ten; even the establishment in 1537 of a special magistracy to curb swearing and indecent language. Less alarming but also restricting, the heavy tax on wine and limited hours of its sale, the regular control of the working day by the bell of St Mark's, and the rigorous checking of visitors to the city, all serve to illustrate that liberty and pleasure were not to be understood lightly under Venetian civilization. The censorious attitude of the older generation who dominated everything emerges most clearly in the essay *On the Sober Life*, which Alvise Cornaro wrote when he was eighty. He described how he gave up drinking and excessive eating when in his thirties, as a *roué* reformed, and boasted of the joys to be had from a self-denying life of family virtue. 'I feel like God the Father with my nephews and grandchildren,' he declared immodestly: 'Sobriety makes the senses purged, the body light, the intellect clear, the mind happy, the memory tenacious, the movements brisk, and the actions prompt.' He certainly prospered: a *terraferma* proprietor who improved his estates scientifically.

It is easy to be beguiled by the Venice which Pietro Aretino evoked, sensuous and bustling, with its lingering sunsets described in the manner of a painting by his friend Titian. Aretino's lodgings overlooked the Rialto Bridge, always one of the busiest and most crowded parts of the city; the regimented and puritanical sides of Venetian life eluded him. In some ways Venice is, and presumably was, one of the less characteristically 'Mediterranean' cities; for much of the time it is not – in spite of popular belief – a place of brilliant light and turbulent animation. The grey Istrian stone and even the marble present an effect of peculiar gloom beneath a pallid sky in a climate which is often cold, wet, or foggy.

88 Bystanders in the Piazza S. Marco; detail from a painting by Gentile
Bellini.

89 Commercial street scene near the Rialto Bridge; detail from a painting by Carpaccio.

'What would there be to live for were it not for literature?' Bernardo Bembo wrote at the beginning of his commonplace book. Had he gone round the assembled greater council asking this rhetorical question, he might have received some short if not coarse replies. For it is clear that neither he nor Francesco Barbaro, that sententious Venetian Cicero, nor his more famous son Pietro Bembo, were altogether typical patricians, in their scholarly cultivation of the literary arts and their close acquaintance with Florentine literary circles. In spite of Petrarch's visit and lingering influence, the new wave of 'humanist' Latin and Greek scholarship, with its effects upon neo-Latin and Italian literature, political values and personal morals, had been slow to advance in Venice. Manuel Chrysoloras had not been appreciated there as he was in Florence. 147

Manuel had written to Coluccio Salutati, chancellor of Florence, reminding him how highly the Romans had valued Greek learning. Florentine would-be Romans, not Venetian, invited him to come and lecture to them in 1397: yet at the same time Athens itself was under Venetian rule. Francesco Barbaro evidently felt one of a small minority persecuted by the philistines, and had to be consoled by Chrysoloras's pupil, Guarino of Verona. In a letter of June 1408 Guarino told him not to be put off learning by men who believed that in the modern world making money was the only worthwhile pursuit; for this, Guarino added with his usual strain of caesaristic authority, they ought to be put in prison.

Nevertheless, during the fifteenth century, the 'humanist' studies, particularly the study of Latin rhetoric, were pursued with zeal by a growing number of Venetian patricians and citizens, as they were in other parts of Italy. From 1414 to 1418, Guarino himself was teaching in Venice, starting his school in the house of Francesco Barbaro, and influencing a growing circle of talented young patricians, Leonardo Giustinian, Fantino Zorzi, Andrea Zulian and others, among them Barbaro's own nephews. 'I have heard that these young patricians here, including yourself, are taking wonderfully to the study of the best arts and letters and polished learning and are ardent and dedicated,' Francesco Barbaro wrote in 1437 to the doge's nephew, Jacopo Foscari, gratified that his own example was being followed. The influence of such studies upon the ethos of patrician administration has been illustrated in an earlier chapter; the virtues of the active political life were repeatedly stressed in Venice as in Florence, even if the special praises of the régime were to be uttered by foreigners, such as Poggio, George of Trebizond and Sabellicus. The prestige attached to classical Latin style and literary allusion is illustrated by the establishment, between 1444 and 1450, of a special school attached to the chancery. Free lectures continued to be given there by distinguished scholars, and descriptive accounts of Venice include this institution as one of the notable sights and amenities of the city, as they included the great library of cardinal Bessarion, bequeathed to St Mark in 1468. It is not surprising that among the works first printed in Venice (by 1471) was Cicero's dialogue *De Oratore*.

These educational developments coincided in time with the rapid political expansion of Venice on the Italian mainland, and the annexation of Verona and Padua may have made the Venetian patriciate more conscious of the scholarly tradition as well as the Roman remains of these cities. It would be disrespectful to the University of Padua to suggest that all its scholarship, whether in arts or sciences, suddenly became Venetian after 1405, and individual Venetians had been connected with Paduan learning long before this date, as had individuals from all over Christendom. Nevertheless, taking over the honours of Padua is implied by the decree of 1407 that in future Venetians should study at no other university, even though Venice had its own first school of natural philosophy established at Rialto the following year. The 'new Roman' type of patrician was gladly drawn to the Roman city nearest Venice; Francesco Barbaro attended Gaspare Barzizza's lectures in Padua; the Bembos, father and son, had a house there, as did many other 'humanist' patricians.

90 Pietro Bembo.

149

The empire *da mar* also had its part to play in the advancement of studies, in particular of Greek, which until the fifteenth century had not been much encouraged in Padua (the first chair of Greek there was created in 1463 for Demetrius Chalcondyles of Athens). The practical advantage to Venetian administrators and businessmen in knowing Greek, since they were so involved with the Greek-speaking world, may have had something to do with this, though it can probably be exaggerated. Guarino was hired by a patrician as secretary and translator in Constantinople, which gave him the opportunity to follow Chrysoloras there in 1400, and Zaccaria Trevisan took Greek lessons when captain of Candia in 1403–04; but Venetians had managed to deal with Greeks for long enough without needing much knowledge of the language of Homer or Pericles, which cannot have been of much use in ordinary communication. In fact, the (citizen) chancellor in Crete from 1388 to 1429, Lorenzo de' Monaci, was one of the strongest opponents to the humanist cultivation of ancient Greek. It was erudite and courteous of Francesco Barbaro and Leonardo Giustinian to have greeted the Byzantine emperor, Manuel Paleologos, with speeches in Greek when he visited Venice in 1423, but not strictly necessary or advantageous, except that it reminded the doge and senate of their superior power over his decayed empire, and their own posture as the civilized 'new Romans'.

The importance to learning of Venetian connections with Greece would seem to lie elsewhere, in that Venice tended to be the place of resort for scholarly Greeks coming west, not just a substitute for Constantinople but the true imperial capital for those coming from Crete and other places. Francesco Barbaro's protégé, George of Trebizond, came from Crete in 1417, and the latter's translation of Plato's *Laws*, which he compared to Venetian practice (1459), earned him a place as a teacher in the chancery school. Among others from Crete were Andronikos Callistes, friend of the Florentine exile Palla Strozzi, who made his home in Venice after 1434, and Marcus Musurus, who succeeded to the chair in Padua in 1503 and subsequently to a

91 Pietro Aretino, painted as a patrician, by Titian.

new chair in Venice itself, which he held from 1512 to 1517.

The presence in Venice of scribes, who had been trained in Crete by the Byzantine exile Michael Apostolis, had a special importance for early printing of Greek. Aldo Manuzio, from near Rome, set up his press in Venice and made a start with the Greek grammar of Constantine Lascaris in 1494–95; although the Aldine press was neither the first nor the only one printing in Greek, it was much the most successful. With Marcus Musurus as his principal editor and proof-reader, and a group of learned patricians as literary advisers and patrons, Aldo made Venice the leading source in the west for the knowledge and diffusion of Greek literature. Texts in the original of the works not only of Homer, Plato, Aristotle and Plutarch, but of writers who had hardly been known before – the historian Thucydides, the dramatist Sophocles and the poet Pindar, for example – all flowed from the Aldine press. Nor was reading ancient Greek literature enough for the impassioned group of young patricians, Pietro Bembo, Angelo Gabriel, Andrea Navagero and others who founded their *Neakademia* with Aldo in 1500; they even insisted on speaking its language in their symposia.

Printed editions not only of Greek, but of Latin and Italian literature, were issued on such a scale in Venice that it has been estimated that over half of all the known books printed in Italy before 1500 came from there. The Aldine press, with its revolutionary emphasis upon text rather than commentary, upon elegant typography with Roman characters based on the humanist 'italic' script, and its production of 'pocket' as well as *de luxe* editions, contributed most to making Venice the great publishing capital, which it remained, even after the censorship or licensing system was introduced in 1527.

The original urge to recover and re-edit classical texts may have been fostered less in Venice than elsewhere in Italy, but in the context of printing, the analogy of Venice with Rome or Athens (Aldo seems to have preferred the latter in some of his prefaces) was justly earned. Indeed, it is most improbable that so large a quantity of literature had ever before been communicated in so short a time from a single city. How far it was communicated within that city is another question; it is not at all clear how much an adequate primary, to say nothing of an elementary education, was available to the majority of those inhabiting Venice and the Venetian empire. The chancery school and academic sessions in patrician houses were obviously for the few. No doubt religious houses and notaries gave instruction, but it was only in 1551 that provision was made for a special tax which would pay masters of grammar to teach in each of the six wards of the city, and this does not tell us very much about popular literacy. Some of the ample funds of the *scuole grandi* or the procurators of St Mark might have been better spent on providing education.

The original literature produced by the patrician and citizen *élite* of Venice, trained in both the ancient classics and those of fourteenth-century Florence (Dante, Petrarch and Boccaccio), tended to be derivative and ponderous, more Roman in spirit perhaps than the literature of the Romans. Pietro Bembo,

92 Colophon used by the Aldine press.   93 Aldo Manuzio.

most eloquent spokesman of this literary world in the early
sixteenth century, declared that all he wanted was a modest
comfort and not dishonourable freedom to pursue the study of
letters, 'always my most vital food for thought'. Bembo also fed
upon social and amorous opportunities, and found his modest
comfort and not dishonourable freedom in the service of the
Church rather than in Venetian commercial and political life;
but the sort of literary food he regurgitated was imitative, and
proudly so. He produced pseudo-Platonic dialogues, pseudo-
Ciceronian prose, pseudo-Petrarchan poetry and letters, and
continued the pseudo-Livian history of Sabellicus; he insisted
on the need for rigid correctness and verbal pedantries in the
use of both classical Latin and a classicized Italian of old-
fashioned Tuscan provenance. Fortunately, he did not attempt a
pseudo-Virgilian epic, an 'Antenoriad' for example; unfortunately, perhaps, his taste or political courage were not suited
to attempting satires of Venetian life in the manner of Juvenal
or Martial, as even Petrarch had done about the papal court of

Avignon. There may have been worthy intention, linguistic skill and a genuinely evocative genius behind the literary pursuits of Bembo, Navagero, Sperone Speroni and other such Augustan figures, but it is not surprising that before the middle of the sixteenth century some of the best-selling works printed in Venice were those of Pietro Aretino, Anton Francesco Doni and other (non-Venetian) writers, who ridiculed *Bembismo* and the erudite assumptions which lay behind it.

It is the lack of a self-critical literature, relating either to the personal or collective experience of Venetian life, which is most regrettable. The fear of criminal prosecution was strong; not even Aretino, the nearest to a Lucian or a Petronius in Venice, dared to vent his astringency upon anything Venetian, apart from clergy, women and the literary forms established by Bembo. The solemn want of wit in Pietro Contarini's *Pleasure Argosy* (1541), a mock epic which consisted of a eulogy of Venetian institutions in the manner of a versified Sabellicus, helps one to understand the poverty of a patrician imagination which could take its neo-Roman pretences so seriously. Of their efforts at writing history, the most striking were not meant for publication; they include the private chronicle diaries kept by Girolamo Priuli, and the 'diaries' or materials for a history of his own time compiled by Marin Sanudo. The polished historical writing in Latin is not very enlightening; not even Paolo Paruta, who at last broke into Italian in official historiography, displays the cutting edge, the breadth of perception or the reasoned pessimism of the Florentines Machiavelli and Guicciardini.

Perhaps there is direct and enjoyable comedy to be found in dialect literature, anonymous lyrics and pasquinades, or the farcical theatre of Ruzzante in Padua; but the massive apparatus of humanist learning and the whole background of Venetian metropolis and empire seem to have produced very little in the way of intelligent self-scrutiny or ridicule. The nearest approach to it may lie in the whimsical *Hypnerotomachia Polifili* of Francesco Colonna, a Dominican friar (descended from an

154

94 Illustration from Francesco Colonna's *Hypnerotomachia* ▶

obscure citizen family) of S. Giovanni e Paolo. Colonna almost
certainly took his own classical learning very seriously, but his
book is so absurd a mixture of fantasy and pedantry, with its
deliberate confusion of the vernacular and ancient languages,
arcane imagery and bizarre descriptions of imaginary ancient
monuments and pagan ceremonies, that it almost seems a
parody of the erudite endeavours and antiquarian allegories of
the pompous age of doge Agostino Barbarigo (1486–1501).
Though the story of the lover's dream upon which all this is
built appears to have been composed before 1470, the greater
part of the work is thought to have been written during the
years 1485–95. Even if Colonna (known to have been no clois-
tered recluse) was in earnest, the possibility remains that Aldo
Manuzio, who published the book in 1499, saw it in a satirical
light; it is certainly difficult to believe that the woodcuts
illustrating the work were not meant to be humorous. The
Hypnerotomachia attains a level of absurdity which the literal
'new Roman' minds of a Marin Sanudo or a Pietro Bembo
could hardly have conceived, though some patricians may have
taken it as a joke. Sanudo recorded in one of his unpublished
lists of Venetian curiosities that a favourite catch-phrase of
Zorzi Emo when he spoke in the senate was 'words of Polifilo!'
to describe long-winded verbiage. In general, though, the
Hypnerotomachia was probably enjoyed less as a satirical work
than as a fantasy, another sincerely nostalgic attempt to re-
create the world of antiquity.

ART: THE IMPERIAL DIADEM

Buildings, sculpture and painting remain the best-known and
most admired relics of Venetian civilization. Their relevance to
the theme of the 'Imperial Age' has been illustrated already,
and the present chapter can offer no adequate appreciation of
them, only some further allusions.

These arts owed less to the patricians than most other aspects
of Venetian life. Though Jacopo de' Barbari bore a patrician
name, this was probably from courtesy or adoption; no mem-

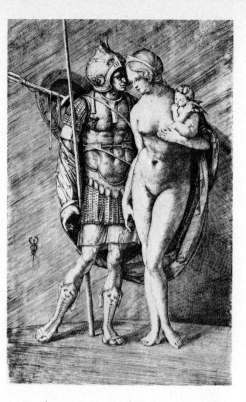

95 Mars and Venus, an engraving by Jacopo de' Barbari.

ber of the ruling caste appears to have practised as an artist. The patrician contribution lay in patronage, but religious bodies, lay fraternities and others, including the independent princely courts of Ferrara and Mantua, also gave many commissions.

Foreigners as well as provincials of the *terraferma* and the *stato da mar* came to work in the Venetian metropolis: Venice was in this way more comparable to papal Rome than to Florence, where there were more numerous local workshops and talent was drawn from a smaller region. Just as in Venice itself some of the art produced had little that was intrinsically 'Venetian' about it, so within the confines of the Venetian empire various independent artistic traditions flourished (as at Padua, for example). It is therefore rather difficult to limit the meaning of 'Venetian art': in its broadest sense this term could cover all art produced within the region of Venetian domination and patronage.

The leading 'Venetian' sculptors and architects of this period came from outside Venice. Inevitably, the Florentine influence was powerful. It was personally expressed in the work of Niccolò di Pietro Lamberti, who came to Venice in *c.* 1415, in that of Donatello who was at Padua *c.* 1443–54, and of Jacopo Sansovino who made his home in Venice after 1527. But there were also some distinguished artists from the *terraferma*. A group of sculptor-architects came from the valleys behind Bergamo: Mauro Coducci, Bartolomeo Buon and the Solari family, Pietro and his sons Tullio and Antonio (known as the Lombardi). Antonio Bregno came from near Como, just beyond the western frontier of Venetian territory, and Antonio Rizzo from Verona. Two great architects of the sixteenth century, Michele Sanmicheli and Palladio, came respectively from Verona and Padua, though Palladio's closest links were to be with Vicenza.

Painting, however, is the art for which Venetian civilization is most celebrated, and here the workshops of Venice itself did exert a characteristic and radiant influence of their own. Yet in this art, too, much was contributed by outsiders. In the 1420s,

96 Idealized femininity: the Dresden Venus, by Giorgione.

97 Giorgione's *Tempesta*, one of the most perplexing examples of a *poesia* painting.

98 *Jacob and Rachel* by Palma il Vecchio: a pastoral scene evoking an Arcadian *terraferma*.

Gentile da Fabriano had been commissioned to decorate the hall of the greater council; later Andrea del Castagno and Giovanni d'Alemagna came to work in Venice, later still Antonello da Messina and Albrecht Dürer. There were also painters of the Venetian *terraferma* who preserved their own styles, such as Pisanello of Verona, Montagna of Vicenza, Cima of Conegliano and Jacopo da Ponte of Bassano, or who assimilated only some Venetian characteristics. Yet the domination of the metropolis was very strong in painting. It is also remarkable how few Venetian or even Venetian-provincial painters, unlike the Florentine, worked outside their own region of Italy. The exceptions are rare: Carlo Crivelli and Lorenzo Lotto, who spent parts of their lives working in the papal state of the Marche, Sebastiano del Piombo and (for a short while) Titian, who worked in Rome; finally, the perverse Jacopo de' Barbari, who went north and almost turned himself into a German painter.

99 *Votive Picture of the Pesaro family* (1519–26) by Titian ▶

LIBERTAS · ECCLESIASTICA

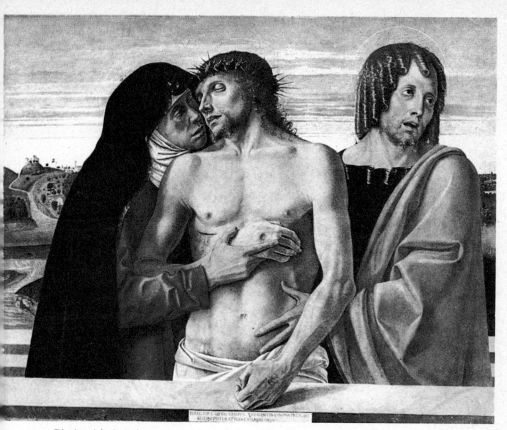

101 Pietà with St John: an early work by Giovanni Bellini (c. 1470).

The special characteristics of Venetian painting lay in the use of colour and light, rather than in the invention and design associated with the Florentines. Long before the end of the fifteenth century these qualities were most celebrated in the works of Jacopo Bellini's sons, Gentile (d. 1506) and Giovanni (d. 1516). Their urban Venetian disciples included Vittorio Carpaccio, Giovanni Mansueti, Vincenzo Catena and Sebastiano del Piombo. But they also attracted provincial painters from all directions; among these were Cariani and Lotto of Bergamo, Marco Basaiti (possibly the son of a Greek) from Friuli, and Schiavone from Dalmatia; most celebrated were the two young men who aspired to take the place of Giovanni Bellini in his old

163

◀ 100 Carlo Crivelli, *The Annunciation* (1486).

102 Vincenzo Catena, *St Jerome in his study*.

age, Giorgione (d. 1510) from Castelfranco and Titian from Cadore, through whom the tradition passed on to Veronese. Even the works of that other great Venetian, Tintoretto (d. 1594), emotionally intense, restless and heretical by the standards of this school, were in their reaction related to it; his daring effects were achieved by use of the same favourite mediums of colour and light in which the Bellini and their followers, especially Titian, so excelled. Why this pursuit of chromatic beauty should have become the special characteristic of Venetian painting is hard to say, apart from its being a local tradition in mosaic and other forms of decoration, which the Bellini and many others enriched. The argument that Venetian light and Venetian skies determined it seems very spurious; the luminous

103 Tintoretto, *Christ before Pilate* ▶

104 Tintoretto, *Miracle of St Mark freeing the slave* (1548).

world of these painters existed mainly in their imaginations, and Guardi in the eighteenth century represented his often cloudy and sombre surroundings rather more truthfully. The argument that they created colour to compensate for actuality's gloomy dullness is scarcely more convincing.

Venetian art was concerned with much else besides the evocation and imitation of antiquity, or the commemoration of the 'new Rome's' splendours; nevertheless, it was here that its achievements were so much more eloquent than in literature, and in the present context these must be the themes most closely considered.

The echoes of ancient art were perhaps most directly captured in sculpture, where the native traditions of Venice were least

105 Titian, *The mocking of Christ* ▶

106, 107 Antonio Rizzo's Adam and Eve.

persistent. Commemorative medals and bronze figurines, the speciality of Donatello's pupil at Padua, Andrea Briosco ('Il Riccio'), were highly fashionable and deliberately imitative of ancient models; while sculpture in stone had begun to abandon 'gothic' for more classically inspired forms by the middle of the fifteenth century. Where the point of departure came is difficult to say; the change is already suggested by the carvings of the Lamberti and other Florentines on the outside of the doge's palace, and the mouldings, figures and cherubs by Bartolomeo Buon on the Porta della Carta: these may reflect the influence of the Florentine bronze-work of Ghiberti and Donatello and possibly of the stone sculpture at Bologna of the Sienese Jacopo della Quercia. Monumentally designed tombs in the great conventual churches of the Frari (Franciscan) and S. Giovanni e Paolo (Dominican) proclaim the triumph of the classical. Andrea Bregno's shield-bearing warriors on the otherwise old-fashioned tomb of doge Foscari, and Pietro Lombardo's military statue on a sarcophagus commemorating the naval hero Jacopo Marcello, were succeeded by the other grand works of the Lombardi, dignified by their disciplined architecture and solemnly poised figure sculptures. The tombs of doges Nicolò Tron, Pietro Mocenigo and Andrea Vendramin are more suggestive of the Roman triumph of fame over death than the Christian triumph of resurrection.

Relief-carving was one of the forms of their art in which the Lombardi particularly excelled, and this was not confined to panels on the tombs. Antonio Lombardo's Miracles of St Anthony in Padua, and Tullio Lombardo's panel of the

108 Rizzo's Nicolò Tron monument in S. Maria dei Frari was begun in 1476, three years after Tron's death.

109 Andrea Vendramin monument by Tullio Lombardo in S. Giovanni e Paolo, completed in the mid 1490s.

Coronation of the Virgin in the church of S. Giovanni Crisostomo, or his illusionistic scenes on the outside of the Scuola of S. Marco, were considered so remarkable that the Paduan Pomponius Gauricus asked in his treatise *De Sculptura* (1504): 'Is not past genius, are not past miracles returned?' Such a nostalgic, antiquarian valuation was the highest praise which could be bestowed in the early sixteenth century. Cardinal Zeno (d. 1501) had wanted his epitaph and tomb in St Mark's 'to be as close as possible to the antique'; even the winged lion on a free-standing column in Vicenza was considered by Luigi da Porto to be 'as beautiful as any of the most famous sculptures of the ancients': he deplored its being broken in 1509 on these aesthetic grounds and not because of the insult to Venice.

Sculpture being, of all the ancient arts, the one of which most fragments still remained, antique busts, torsos, figurines, medals and the like were avidly sought by Venetians; the inventory of Pietro Bembo's collection in Padua suggests a marked preference for these over contemporary art. 'Good has sprung from this evil of the Sack of Rome,' Pietro Aretino declared when the Florentine sculptor-architect Jacopo Sansovino moved to Venice; Aretino ordered him to make a copy of the Laocoön. Sculpture in Venice had attained a high level of art with the Lombardi, but somehow it did not develop much beyond their creative imitation of the antique. Florentines were responsible for the most imaginative feats of sculpture: Donatello's altarpiece and equestrian statue of Gattamelata in Padua, Verrocchio's Colleoni (though this was finished by the Venetian goldsmith, Alessandro Leopardi) and the many figures by Sansovino, including his Michelangelo-like Neptune and Mercury.

In architecture, the gradual replacement in the later fifteenth century of the florid curvilinear traditions by the Vitruvian orders, proportion and symmetry, has been mentioned already in different contexts. There were the double columns of the Arsenal gateway (1460) as an early example, and the courtyard of the doge's palace where, after the fire of 1483, Antonio

110 Titian's portrait
of Jacopo Strada,
an antique dealer
(1567–68).

111 Lorenzo Lotto's
portrait of
Andrea Odoni (1527).

112 S. Zaccaria.   113 S. Michele in Isola.

Rizzo, who designed the great staircase, preserved only one of the pointed arch arcades. Nevertheless, many buildings designed with a deliberate Roman allusion retained much that was indigenously Venetian. Mauro Coducci's S. Michele in Isola, the first church to display the new style (started 1469), was acclaimed by the literary monk Pietro Delfino as 'a temple which not only equals antiquity but improves on it'. None the less, the lunette shape dominating the upper façade of S. Michele is unlike anything in Roman architecture. Some scholars think Coducci copied it from Alberti's plans for the Malatesta Temple at Rimini or from the cathedral of Sebenico (the latter case, in Dalmatia, would illustrate that art in a subject city could be ahead of the metropolis). Alternatively, it might have been meant as an echo of the façade of St Mark's. Coducci repeated it upon the façade of S. Zaccaria, the Scuola of S. Marco, and S. Giovanni Evangelista, and the church of S. Giovanni Crisostomo; and it recurs in numerous other buildings. The Venetian decorative tradition also survived in the use of surface colour.

114 Ca' d'Oro. 115 Palazzo Corner (Ca' Grande).

Although Ca' d'Oro (1421–31), a private house built for Marin Contarini, was the climax and finale of gilded flamboyance, over fifty years later the house of Giovanni Dario, a prominent citizen, still retained polychrome patterns upon the walls, in spite of its very different window mouldings: so did Pietro Lombardo's design for the tiny sanctuary church of S. Maria dei Miracoli (1481–89).

Giorgione's vanished paintings on the walls of the Fondaco dei Tedeschi are another reminder that the blankness of Istrian stone was not wholly prevalent. Nevertheless, a more Roman orthodoxy was Coducci's aim in the arcaded block he designed for the procurators of St Mark and in the house he planned for the Loredan family (Ca' Loredan-Vendramin-Calergi) with its heavy cornice and use of columns and pilasters. Other town-houses developed the new forms, culminating in Jacopo Sansovino's majestic Ca' Corner (called Ca' Grande) with its correct use of the Vitruvian orders, and rusticated ground or water storey. Sansovino, Gianmaria Falconetto, Michele

173

Sanmicheli and Andrea Palladio, made architecture a peculiarly expressive form for the empire and Roman pretensions of Venice in the sixteenth century, from urban palaces and fortifications to rural villas. There had been many imitations of the campanile of St Mark, and Candia (Heraklion), the capital of Crete, had long possessed its own St Mark's and ducal palace: now even smaller places, Dalmatian towns like Sebenico and Lesina, were imitating the capital with simpler copies of Sansovino's *loggetta*, or, as in Padua, clock-towers on the Venetian model. Civic buildings were embellished almost everywhere under Venetian rule, perhaps the most impressive reconstruction being that of the Council Hall (Palazzo della Ragione) in Vicenza which Palladio, who began his improvements in 1549, renamed with Vitruvian fervour 'The Basilica'. Above all, the fortresses and strengthened city walls with their gateways like triumphal arches, in Verona, Padua, Belluno and elsewhere, manifested the mastery of the winged lion.

116 Far left, Palladio's Loggia del Capitanato, Vicenza; the surface decoration commemorates the victory at Lepanto.

117 Above left, Palazzo dei Rettori (begun 1491) and clock-tower, Belluno.

118 Above, clock-tower, Padua.

119 Porta San Tomaso, Treviso (1518).

120 Right, Porta Savonarola, Padua (1530), designed by Gianmaria Falconetto.

122 Palladio's attempt to re-create a Roman house in Venice: cloister for the canons of the Carità (1552).

121 Andrea Mantegna's *Triumph of Scipio*, painted for Francesco Cornaro.

In some respects there were fewer 'new Roman' allusions in Venetian painting than in sculpture and architecture; Florentine painters were more preoccupied with antiquity, more concerned to study nature through classical form, geometry and anatomy, and nostalgic even to the point of trying to re-create lost ancient paintings from literary description. Colourful extemporizing was the essential Venetian tradition, and a delight in landscape which was more romantic than precise in its suggestion of the subalpine scenery of the *terraferma* and the rocky coasts of Dalmatia. Yet Dürer complained in 1506 to his friend Pirkheimer that Venetian painters criticized his works as 'not good because they are not antique art'.

Exactly what Dürer's critics meant is not quite clear; they may have meant various things, for the art of the Bellini workshop had made a variety of references to 'antique art'. Evocative sketches of Roman architectural forms, sculpture and inscriptions filled pages of Jacopo Bellini's later book of drawings (*c.* 1450); Giovanni Bellini's early painting, *The Blood of the*

177

Redeemer (mid 1460s), shows behind the figure of Christ a parapet with relief scenes in 'antique' style, while antiquarian bric-à-brac and 'painted sculpture' were characteristic of many pictures by his brother-in-law Andrea Mantegna, whose art derived from Padua in a separate tradition. Later in his career, Giovanni Bellini developed more subtle forms of allusion: portraiture based on the head and shoulders as in an ancient bust; balanced and reposeful compositions of figures in an architectural setting, which are most perfectly illustrated by his S. Zaccaria altarpiece (1505). There was also the genre of painting allegories, based on ancient myth, sometimes fairly obvious ones, sometimes very esoteric and mixed in their literary sources, such as the so-called *Feast of the Gods* which Bellini finished painting for the duke of Ferrara in 1514, or Titian's accompanying *Bacchus and Ariadne* and other works.

123 Titian, *Bacchus and Ariadne*.

124 Giovanni Bellini,
S. Zaccaria
altarpiece (1505).

Such 'literary' painting had been fashionable enough in Florence in the fifteenth century; Aldo Manuzio's printed edition of Ovid's *Metamorphoses* (1497) and other publications, including Sannazaro's *Arcadia* in 1502, may have widened the taste for it in Venice.

Yet a more romantic dimension of this was devised by the genius of the aged Bellini and the young Giorgione in the early sixteenth century, cognate with the strange fantasy world of the *Hypnerotomachia*. This was the *poesia* in its purest sense, which Pietro Bembo explained in a letter of January 1506 to Bellini's would-be patroness, Isabella d'Este, wife of the marquis of Mantua: 'he does not like to be given many written details which cramp his style; his way of working, as he says, is always to wander at will in his pictures so that they can give satisfaction to himself as well as to the beholder'. It was in this spirit that Giorgione worked, creating for his enraptured patrician patrons a pastoral golden age, vaguely alluding to the poetry of Theocritus and Virgil, but full of imaginative enigmas which were not meant to instruct or illustrate so much as give delight.

An art which provided fame-assuring portraits and evocative fantasies for patrician patrons, religious themes serenely, dramatically or descriptively composed for churches, monastic houses and the *scuole grandi*, testified in rich variety to the 'Roman' myth of Venice. Some paintings might convey patriotic achievement, piety and immortalizing portraiture all at once, as did Titian's *Madonna di Ca' Pesaro* (1519–26): Benedetto Pesaro is here presented to the Virgin by St Peter, in honour of his conquest of Cephalonia and Santa Maura from the Turks in 1502, watched devoutly by his family. The greatest examples of such monumental painting must have been the Bellini workshop's narrative scenes in the hall of the greater council (replacing those by Gentile da Fabriano and Pisanello). These have all perished, but we have the narrative scenes, completed in 1500 for the Scuola of S. Giovanni Evangelista, Gentile Bellini's picture of the recovery of the relic of the True Cross by the grand guardian Andrea Vendramin, and the accompanying scenes of miracles wrought by this relic, painted by Carpaccio and others, which portray the whole of Venetian society in a drama of pious endeavour and fulfilment.

Art enhanced the pose of Venice as a holy and apostolic city most splendidly in the mosaic and sculptural decoration of St Mark's basilica, but religious painting in the sixteenth century cast another challenge in the direction of Rome, in terms of artistic primacy. Titian's seated St Mark, painted *c.* 1512 for the monastery of Santo Spirito in Isola, is as imperious as any St Peter; his Frari altarpiece of the Assumption, Veronese's mural and canvas paintings in S. Sebastiano, and Tintoretto's masterpieces for the two *scuole grandi* of S. Marco and S. Rocco, replied with a marvellous originality and power to the celebrated decorations in the Vatican of Raphael and Michelangelo.

125 Titian,
St Mark enthroned
(*c.* 1512).

Something has been said in earlier chapters about the use of art to express Venetian authority and grandeur. Perhaps the patrician self-importance and new-Roman make-believe were never more vividly expressed than in the enormous, voluptuously colourful canvases of Veronese: above all in the series of scriptural dinner-parties which he painted for monastic refectories. The *Wedding at Cana*, the feasts in the House of Levi and of Simon the Pharisee were portrayed as opulent patrician banquet scenes; the *Supper of St Gregory the Great to the Poor* and the *Supper at Emmaus* introduced humbler company, but still in the splendid setting of enormous fluted columns, elegant balconies, staircases and pediments beneath tranquil skies, scenery essential to the charade of resumed Roman grandeur.

181

126 Veronese, *Feast in the House of Levi* (1560) ▶

The state commissions to artists remain, nevertheless, the most direct memorials of empire: the innumerable lions of St Mark, the personifications of Justice, the new civic buildings and the allegorical and historical scenes painted in the doge's palace. Of the latter, most grandiose if not perhaps most beautiful, was Veronese's *Apotheosis of Venice* in the centre of the ceiling of the hall of the greater council (*c.* 1583): the coronation of a divine empress superimposed on twisted columns reminiscent of the High Altar of St Peter's, Rome. Likewise, the improvements to the Piazza San Marco in the sixteenth century placed a relentless emphasis on imperial themes. Alessandro Leopardi's bronze bases to the flagpoles in front of the basilica, which (according to Francesco Sansovino) symbolized Venice, Cyprus and Crete, the three main pillars of the empire, were covered with political allegories.

More conspicuous and even more elaborate was Jacopo Sansovino's programme of sculptures for his *loggetta* below the campanile (1537–49). Francesco Sansovino recorded his father's highly individual train of thought, beginning with the statue of Pallas. 'The city of Venice has in the course of time superseded all other republics by means of its marvellous government . . . the Ancients portrayed Pallas as personifying wisdom; I wanted this to be an armed Pallas, prompt to act and vigorous, because the wisdom of the Fathers of the Republic in state matters is singular and without equal.' Of the statue of Mercury he had declared, 'all things prudently thought out and arranged

have yet to be expressed with eloquence, and in this Republic eloquence has always had an important place, and eloquent men have been great in number and reputation; therefore I have wanted to represent Mercury as signifying letters and eloquence'. Next he explained, 'the statue of Apollo is the sun, which is singular and unique, just as this Republic, for its constituted laws, its unity, and uncorrupted liberty, is a sun in the world, regulated with justice and wisdom; furthermore, it is known how this nation takes a more than ordinary delight in music, and Apollo signifies music. Moreover, from the union of the magistracies, combined with equable temperament, there arises an unusual harmony, which perpetuates this admirable government: for these reasons was Apollo represented.' He then concluded, 'The last statue is Peace, so much loved by this Republic, and by which it has grown to such greatness and become the metropolis of all Italy.' On relief panels above these figures, Venice appears personified as Justice, with the river gods of the *terraferma* below her, Venus representing Cyprus, and Jupiter representing Crete. Perhaps there is no work of art, not even among the paintings in the doge's palace, which celebrates the self-importance and antique nostalgia of imperial Venice more eloquently than this.

127, 128, 129 Relief sculpture on the *loggetta*. In the centre is Venice as Justice, with the river gods of the *terraferma*. To the left is Jupiter, personifying Crete, and to the right Venus, personifying Cyprus.

This essay has been concerned with the heyday of Venetian civilization, not with the inexhaustible subject of its decline. The 'decline' of Venice does not in any case have much general or objective meaning. In Ruskin's opinion architectural and moral decline were already beginning in the first half of the fifteenth century; many historians, from Machiavelli onwards, have associated political decline with the League of Cambrai war when Venice was humbled as a European power; demographers and historians of government, society and art find convincing evidence of decline in the seventeenth century; while economic historians distinguish a long series of setbacks, adaptations and recoveries: Venice was not rising, but on the other hand not sinking, even in the hundred years before its surrender to Napoleon (1797). Nevertheless, in most respects it is possible to justify taking the end of the sixteenth century as the end of the 'Imperial Age', and to argue that there was in many ways a recession of Venetian civilization developing during and after the 1570s.

The contrast with the previous decade, when Venice and the Venetian empire had their highest population and trade figures recorded, is at once dramatic. The Turkish war of 1570–73, immensely expensive, had brought the loss of Cyprus; and between 1575 and 1577 recurrent plague destroyed about a third of the city's population – figures as catastrophic as those of the mid fourteenth-century mortality. It is tempting to take as symbolic events the death from plague of Titian, who as Giovanni Bellini's successor had seen, served and expressed Venetian civilization since the beginning of the century, or the fires which broke out in the doge's palace in 1574 and 1577, destroying a vast amount of the archives of the republic as well

◀ 130 Justice above the piazzetta wall of the doge's palace: one of the two statues by Alessandro Vittoria (1579).

as the historical decorations by the Bellini brothers and their assistants in the hall of the greater council.

The isolation of such events as these is, however, facile; deeper forces directed the tide of recession. In 1501, only twelve years after annexation, the then governor or *luogotenente* of Nicosia had described Cyprus as vital to the Venetian empire and its preservation – much the same as had been said about Negroponte in 1470. Yet the Venetian empire had flourished before it acquired Cyprus and after it lost Negroponte; it was not necessarily doomed even after the fall of Famagusta to the Turks and the horrible martyrdom of its defender Marcantonio Bragadin. Though the Holy League formed in August 1571 was too late to retrieve the island, it won in October the naval victory of Lepanto. Much of the credit went to the Venetian commander Sebastiano Venier, and the immediate effect of his success was a prolonged and varied season of jubilation in Venice; in the most ambitious pageant described, the figure of Victory rode upon a bleeding serpent, a symbol of evil curiously reminiscent of the Visconti viper, that other scourge over whom the Venetians had prevailed. The long-term effect of Lepanto was that Turkish power made no more conquests of Venetian dominion for over three generations.

After the plague of the 1570s, the recorded population was never quite so high as before, but there was a remarkable recovery, just as there had been after the fourteenth- and fifteenth-century plagues. A census of 1581 gave the figure of 134,871 (still very much higher than estimates in the earlier part of the century) and in 1624 it exceeded 140,000. This is not enough to discount altogether the horrors of the epidemic, some of whose effects on mainland as well as urban manpower seem to have been far-reaching, but it modifies the idea of cataclysm. The symbolic events can be dismissed more quickly: Titian was, after all, a very old man in 1576; the doge's palace, which had suffered badly from fires in the fifteenth century, was rebuilt exactly as before (Palladio's proposal to replace it with a neo-classical building was rejected); the workshops of

Veronese and Tintoretto redecorated it with some of the most imperious paintings ever devised.

Did then the events of the 1570s merely repeat the perennial disasters which Venice had survived throughout the whole of this period? Certainly the apparent recovery and continuity were impressive, but the long-term problems of Venice were growing and badly aggravated during this decade.

Within the Mediterranean world Venetian predominance among the Christian powers was clearly decreasing, and the Turkish war itself, rather than the loss of Cyprus, seems to have encouraged the competition. Not only were other ports developing a direct interest in the eastern trade – Marseilles (serving the fairs of Lyons), Ragusa, and Leghorn most conspicuously – but the ships of Atlantic powers were also intruding. The Spanish wars in the Netherlands and the sack of Antwerp (1576) may have benefited Venetian markets in Germany, but they also encouraged English companies to enter directly into the Levantine trade. At the same time, the volume of Venetian registered shipping steadily declined: between 1560 and 1600 it is reckoned to have fallen by half. Shipbuilding, afflicted by short supplies of timber, was ceasing to be a major industry in Venice; adequate crews for the ships were also becoming difficult to find, owing to the plague, and the temptations of higher wages and better working conditions in light industries and crafts. The growth of 'Christian' piracy, even in the upper Adriatic where the 'Uscocchi' (a mixed band of military adventurers and political exiles) controlled the seas round Fiume, was another symptom of the decline of Venetian naval power and the demoralization of Venetian sailors. That foreign-built ships were being used for Venetian merchandise and foreign-owned ships were using the port did not necessarily mean a decline in business; the return to 'protection' in 1602 was much more disastrous. Such evidence does suggest, however, that the figure of Neptune as a patriotic symbol and the ritual of marrying the sea on Ascension Day were little more than vain postures in a world which had changed.

The biggest changes in maritime commerce during the sixteenth century had been oceanic rather than Mediterranean; it was here that Venice was stagnant rather than growing like Seville and Antwerp or (in the seventeenth century) London and Amsterdam. It was not that individual Venetians lacked zeal for exploration and new opportunity, in the tradition of Marco Polo. Leonardo da' Mosto had taken a leading part in the early voyages to West Africa, discovering the mouth of the river Gambia in 1455–56; Antonio Pigafetta of Vicenza returned from a trans-world voyage in 1523; Giovanni Battista Ramusio published many travellers' descriptions of distant places. Collectively, however, neither the will nor the money, nor the convincing advantage, could be found for developing a Venetian East India Company.

The problem had to be faced in 1585 when Philip II of Spain offered Venice the monopoly of the spice trade in Lisbon and Antwerp. There were political difficulties involved in a close association with Spain, but also many economic disadvantages in accepting the offer. It was not clear what goods could be marketed in exchange in Portugal: prices would fall with the abundance of pepper; the Venetian cloth industry which supplied so much to Syria would be ruined; all in all, Venetian capital was tied up with its interests in the eastern Mediterranean, and the conservative patricians were unwilling to risk losing their traditional places in the sun. They rejected Philip II's offer.

Long-distance trade and shipping were not only losing their predominance, but also their undisputed place as the favourite form of investment. The shift of capital to industry, and even to land, when this meant drainage and other improvements to increase home-grown food-supplies, was less serious than the growth of investment in property for security and prestige, rents and only limited agricultural returns. How much the 'Mocenigo doctrine' was being disregarded can be shown by figures: the yield of the land tax trebled between 1537 and 1582, and between 1570 and 1630 it has been reckoned that 35 per cent of patrician income came from mainland estates. The government-aided schemes of Alvise Cornaro and other promoters of massive land improvement seem to have flourished most between 1540 and 1570; shortages of labour and disputes among proprietors then reduced their promise.

In general, there is evidence of change in patrician morale in and after the later decades of the sixteenth century. If many family fortunes had ceased to grow and living standards were at the mercy of rising prices, there were two obvious precautions to take: breed smaller families, and perform less public service. Whether any patrician paterfamilias resolved his problems quite so crudely as this cannot be shown, but the changes in a couple of generations were serious and remarked upon. The numbers of the greater council seem to have been falling from their peak of *c*. 2600 even before 1570, but many patrician families lost men, including heirs, in the period of war and plague (1570–77); between the census of 1563 and that of 1581 there was a drop of nearly 600 patricians, and the numbers only just climbed above 2000 again in the early seventeenth century. At the same time, to conserve inheritances and living standards, marriages were being limited to few (sometimes only one) of a number of sons, and inheritances were entailed so that capital could not be realized and put at risk. Individual patrician families had often died out in the past (merely within the years 1503–19 Sanudo recorded no less than six which became extinct) but overall numbers had risen until the mid sixteenth century. The moral caution which conserved money in property and limited the likely number of patrician sons reduced the supply of patricians willing, wealthy and competent enough to make careers in government service. The effects were only gradually felt over half a century, but by the 1630s they were a serious subject for debate, and in 1646 the greater council was at last opened to new members for payment.

After the first few years of the seventeenth century, this long-maturing crisis had approached its climax. Traditional Venetian commerce suffered new blows. The Dutch and

English, using the Cape route to the Indian Ocean, were capturing the supply, transport and marketing of spices far more thoroughly than the Portuguese had ever done. The Thirty Years War in Germany disturbed overland routes and markets even more seriously than the Spanish domination of non-Venetian Lombardy. The ruinously expensive Turkish war of 1646–69 deprived the republic of Crete, its oldest and most valuable territory in the east. Finally, the great plague of 1630–31 seems to have brought a far larger and more permanent fall in the population than any of the previous epidemics. Longhena's splendid church of S. Maria della Salute stands at the entrance to the Grand Canal as a memorial to the passing of this plague, and other baroque churches and palaces show that architecture at least could still be imaginative and forceful in Venice; but the same could scarcely be said of Venetian literature and painting in the seventeenth century.

It would not have been possible to detect and foresee all this as the processions of 1571 wound their way round the Piazza San Marco, and Gabrieli's triumphal music celebrated the victory of Lepanto. Three years later, Henry III of France came on a state visit which inspired other expensive and patriotic pageants. Neptune personified Venice, attended by the four *terraferma* rivers of Brenta, Adige, Po and Piave; Palladio erected a temporary Roman arch on the Lido. Recessional tides were no more thinkable then than at the time of Queen Victoria's Diamond Jubilee. Not even the most judicious of Venetian historians, Paolo Paruta, was ready yet to suggest that the 'Imperial Age' was over; in his dialogue *On the Perfection of the Political Life* (1579), he affirmed that Venice, greater than Rome, would still have a great future. Evidently some of the chauvinistic self-confidence of the days of doge Agostino Barbarigo still survived in patrician minds, as it did in the paintings for the halls of the doge's palace. Nicolò Contarini looked back with nostalgia to the late 1590s when he began writing his continuation of Venetian history in 1623. 'The

Republic was at that time in the apparent confidence of all

131 Procession celebrating the Holy League (1571).

princes, and open friendship with everyone; moreover, there was an abundance of everything which the fertility of the country, the industry of man, and a suitable site usually yield under well-regulated government.' He continued: 'mercantile commerce flowed from all sides, so that it rendered the city superior in its traffic to any other . . . at the time one really thought that it was perhaps greater than it had ever been before.'

This retrospective optimism was misleading. Contarini himself admitted that the cup of happiness had not been full, because, in his judgment, luxury and idleness had accompanied prosperity. Doge Nicolò Donà went further in a speech made to the senate in 1610, deploring the fact that French cloth traders were underselling the Venetians in Aleppo, and he detected a lack of initiative compared to earlier times: 'in the days before the war with the Turks [1570–73] all was grandeur, utility, emolument, commodity, honour . . . everyone was interested in sea voyages, in business, in everything appertaining to the existence and greater good of the fatherland.' Paruta, preceding Contarini as continuator of the official history of Venice from the time of the League of Cambrai, a work which he began in the 1580s, made his introduction sound apologetic – almost an epitaph for the 'Imperial Age':

The Republic of the Venetians, for the long continuity of its empire and the excellence of its government, may truly be reckoned the fairest and most blessed by fortune of all those the world has ever seen . . . leaving behind all other human cities in memory except one, Rome. Certainly the fact that such a Republic has not acquired an even greater empire should not be attributed to any meanness or weakness among its citizens, but rather to its long-lived equity and modesty. . . . For among our ancestors, most innocent men, it was the custom to undertake war not for lust of domination, but rather in the desire to conserve liberty; wholly intent on the good of the Republic, caring little for their private gain, they strove with great effort to be, not just to appear, good men. Hence it came about that, placing the highest glory not in greatness of empire nor in the praise of others, but in the good government of the city and their own clear consciences, they lost many opportunities to increase the Republic, whence, the city already being made powerful by means of its land forces and naval fleets, appeared to have something of the majesty and grandeur of the ancient Roman name. If more had been done at the right time, the city of Venice would have risen to such a pitch of greatness that for empire and glory in war one could have compared the same Republic to the Republic of Rome.

BIBLIOGRAPHICAL NOTES

A. GENERAL WORKS

Still fundamental are S. Romanin, *Storia documentata di Venezia* (10 vols; 1st ed. Venice 1853–61, 2nd ed. 1912–25), and P. Molmenti, *La storia di Venezia nella vita privata dalle origini alla caduta della Republica* (1st ed. Turin 1880, 6th ed. Bergamo 1922–25). The latter was translated by H. F. Brown as *Venice: Its Individual Growth from the Beginnings to the Fall of the Republic* (3 vols., London 1906). The available works in English are all old. W. C. Hazlitt, *The History of the Origin and Rise of the Venetian Republic* (1st ed. London 1858, 4th ed. 1915), is a reliable old-fashioned political history; F. C. Hodgson, *Venice in the Thirteenth and Fourteenth Centuries* (London 1914), is useful for the earlier period. Shorter introductions in English are H. F. Brown, *Venice: An Historical Sketch of the Republic* (London 1893), and A. Wiel, *Venice* (London 1894). Even older than most of these but perennially stimulating are the remarks (all too few) about Venice and Venetians by Jacob Burckhardt, *The Civilization of the Renaissance in Italy* (trans. S. G. C. Middlemore; many eds.).

There are more recent and important works in Italian, French and German. The former include R. Cessi, *Storia della Republica di Venezia* (Messina 1944–46), G. Luzzatto, *Storia economica di Venezia* (Padua 1961), and the series produced by the Fondazione Giorgio Cini, *Storia della civiltà veneziana* (8 vols., Florence 1955–62) of which see in particular *La civiltà veneziana del Quattrocento* (1957) and *La civiltà veneziana del Rinascimento* (1958). In French there is an attractive short account by F. Thiriet, *Histoire de Venise* (*Que sais-je?* series,

Paris 1952), and in German the more copious work by M. Kretschmayr, *Geschichte von Venedig* (Stuttgart 1934, reprinted 1964).

For topography, monuments and art the two best guide-books remain F. Sansovino, *Venetia città nobilissima et singolare descritta in XIII libri* (Venice 1581; the ed. of 1663, with additions by G. Martinioni, has been reprinted in facsimile, Venice 1968), and G. Lorenzetti, *Venezia ed il suo estuario* (Venice 1926) of which there is an English translation by J. Guthrie: *Venice and its Lagoon. Historical-Artistic Guide* (Rome 1961). The Touring Club Italiano Guides are excellent; see not only *Venezia e i suoi dintorni* but also *Veneto, Friuli e Venezia Giulia* and *Venezia Tridentina*. The *Enciclopedia Italiana* is also valuable for reference.

B. PRIMARY SOURCES

There is a profusion of unpublished documentary material in Venice and elsewhere; printed calendars of records have in general not advanced beyond the fourteenth century. This book contains a number of references to archival sources, e.g. on p. 80 to a register of the greater council (Archivio di Stato, Venice: Maggior Consiglio Deliberazioni Reg. 'Ursa' 1415–54) and on p. 130 to an act book of the Signori di Notte (Signori di Notte al criminale B.15). On pp. 79, 87 there are references to ambassadors' letters from Venice (Archivio di Stato, Mantua: Gonzaga B. 1431; Archivio di Stato, Milan: Ducale, Carteggio Visconteo-Sforzesco Potenze Estere B.1063). Contemporary literary works consulted in manuscript include Bernardo Bembo's commonplace book (British Museum, Additional MSS 41068A) and Marin Sanudo's descriptive lists and notes (Biblioteca Correr, Venice, MSS Cicogna 969–70).

Among the contemporary sources in print, the works of Marin Sanudo deserve first mention. There is an incomplete edition of his description (mentioned above) or *Cronachetta* by R. Fulin (Venice 1880) and a synopsis by the same editor in

Archivio veneto iv (1872) 92–99. Sanudo's mainland tour was edited by R. Brown, *Itinerario per la terraferma nell'anno 1483* (Padua 1847), and see also R. Fulin, 'Frammenti inediti dell' itinerario in terraferma di Marin Sanudo', *Archivio veneto* xxii (1881). The revised edition of Sanudo's *Le vite dei Dogi di Venezia* by G. Monticolo (*Rerum italicarum scriptores* xxii) has not gone beyond Sebastiano Ziani (d. 1178), but it contains the introductory material; for the later biographies Muratori's edition of 1713 must still be used. Sanudo's copious *Diarii* or annals compiled from the official records (58 vols., Venice 1879–1903) remain the outstanding groundwork of a contemporary history. See vol. 58 (ii) for a study of Sanudo's life and works; also G. Cozzi, 'Marin Sanudo il Giovane; della cronaca alla storia', *Rivista storica italiana* lxxx (1968).

The official history of Venice, by Marcantonius Sabellicus, Pietro Bembo, Paolo Paruta and Nicolò Contarini successively, is printed under the title *Degli istorici degli cose veneziane i quali hanno scritto per pubblico decreto* (Venice 1718). Of more interest, however, are the private patrician chronicles; on these, see the remarks of H. Baron, 'A forgotten chronicle of early fifteenth century Venice', *Essays in History and Literature presented to Stanley Pargellis* (Chicago 1965), and F. Thiriet, 'Les chroniques de la Marcienne et leur importance pour l'histoire de la Romanie gréco-vénitienne', *Mélanges d'archéologie et d'histoire de l'École française de Rome* lxvi (1954). Two of the most accessible works are Domenico Malipiero, *Annali veneti 1457–1500*, ed. T. Gar and A. Sagredo (*Archivio storico italiano* 1st ser. vii, 1843), and Girolamo Priuli, *I Diarii*, ed. R. Cessi (*Rerum italicarum scriptores* xxiv, part iii, Bologna 1933–37).

Contemporary literary material which has been cited also includes the autobiography of Giovanni Bembo, ed. T. Mommsen, in *Sitzungsberichte der K. Bayerischen Akad. der Wissenschaften zu München Phil.-Hist. Kl.* (1861), and various letter collections. Among these are *Centotrenta lettere inedite di Francesco Barbaro*, ed. R. Sabbadini (Salerno 1884), and *Epistolario di Guarino Veronese* (Venice 1915–19); G. B. Picotti, 'Le lettere di Ludovico

Foscarini', *L'Ateneo veneto* xxxii (1909); *Lettere Storiche di Luigi da Porto*, ed. B. Bressan (Florence 1857); *Lettere di Pietro Aretino*, ed. F. Nicolini (*Scrittori d'Italia* 53, Bari 1913).

Many works by non-Venetian observers (including travellers) contain passages relevant to Venetian history. See Pius II's 'Commentaries', trans. F. A. Gragg and L. C. Gabel, *Smith College Studies in History* xxii, xxv, xxx, xxxv, xliii (Northampton, Mass. 1937–57), and abridged by the same editors as *Memoirs of a Renaissance Pope* (London 1958); also *Memoirs of Philippe de Commines*, ed. A. R. Scoble (2 vols., London 1855–56). An anonymous French description of Venetian government was printed (incompletely) by P. M. Perret, *Histoire des relations de la France avec Venise du XIIIe siècle à l'avènement de Charles VIII*, vol. ii (Paris 1896). Travellers' descriptions include: M. Letts, *Pero Tafur, Travels and Adventures 1435–9* (London 1926); A. Stewart, *The Book of the Wanderings of Brother Felix Fabri* (Palestine Pilgrims Texts Society, London 1892–93); M. M. Newett, *Canon Casola's Pilgrimage to Jerusalem in 1494* (Manchester 1907); M. de Montaigne, *Journal de voyage en Italie*, ed. C. Dédéyan (Paris 1945); T. Coryate, *Coryat's Crudities* (2 vols., Glasgow 1905).

For Venetian art, the primary sources are, of course, the works themselves, but some documentation of patronage will be found in: P. Paoletti, *L'architettura e la scultura del Rinascimento in Venezia* (2 vols., Venice 1893) and *Raccolta di documenti inediti per servire alla storia della pittura veneziana* (Padua 1894–95); G. Lorenzi, *Monumenti per servire alla storia del Palazzo Ducale* (Venice 1869); G. C. Williamson, *The Anonimo* (London 1903).

C. SECONDARY WORKS

These are arranged under chapter headings, though it will be appreciated that some titles are applicable to more than one chapter.

On the 'myth' of Venice and related themes, see the recent essay by F. Gilbert, 'The Venetian Constitution in Florentine Political Thought' (with valuable footnote references) in *Florentine Studies*, ed. N. Rubinstein (London 1968), and for the beginnings of the 'myth', G. Fasoli, 'Nascita di un mito', *Studi storici in onore di Gioacchino Volpe* i (Florence 1958). For the thirteenth century, see O. Demus, 'A Renascence of early christian art in thirteenth century Venice', *Late classical and mediaeval studies in honour of Albert Matthias Frend Jr* (Princeton 1955). G. Cracco, *Società e stato nel medioevo veneziano* (Venice 1967), provides a stimulating analysis of politics and society to the end of the fourteenth century; unfortunately it is without a bibliography. On humanist influences and their impact upon politics and historiography, see F. Saxl, 'Petrarch and Venice', *Lectures* i (London 1957); H. Baron, 'Cicero and the Roman Civic Spirit', *Bulletin of the John Rylands Library* xxii (1938), and *Humanistic and Political Literature in Florence and Venice at the Beginning of the Quattrocento* (Cambridge, Mass. 1955); G. Zippel, 'Lorenzo Valla e le origini della storiografia umanistica veneziana', *Rinascimento* vii (1956); G. Cozzi, 'Cultura, politica e religione nella pubblica storiografia veneziana del '500', *Bolletino dell'Istituto di Storia e dello Stato Veneziano* vi (1963–64). A recent work which could not be consulted in time for this book is W. J. Bouwsma, *Venice and the Defence of Republican Liberty* (Berkeley, California 1968). On the doge's palace under Agostino Barbarigo, see M. Muraro, 'La scala senza giganti', *De Artibus Opuscula XL: Essays in honour of Erwin Panofsky*, ed. M. Meiss (New York 1961).

II VENETIAN EMPIRE

Still useful as a short introduction in English to Venetian economic policy is H. F. Brown, 'The Commercial and Fiscal Policy of the Venetian Republic', *Studies in Venetian History* i (London 1907), 335–66. However, this field has long been dominated by the works of G. Luzzatto and F. C. Lane. For the former, see besides his *Storia economica di Venezia* (see Section A above) which goes up to the early sixteenth century, his *Studi di storia economica veneziana* (Padua 1954), and F. C. Lane, 'Gino Luzzatto's contributions to the history of Venice', *Nuova Rivista Storica* xlix (1965). Many of F. C. Lane's articles on Venetian trade, finance, shipping and industry have been reprinted in his *Venice and History: Collected Papers of F. C. Lane* (Baltimore 1966); this collection includes 'The Mediterranean Spice Trade: Its Revival in the Sixteenth Century'. See also his *Andrea Barbarigo, Merchant of Venice* (Baltimore 1944), and *Venetian Ships and Shipbuilders of the Renaissance* (Baltimore 1934) of which there is a new French edition, *Navires et Constructeurs à Venise pendant la Renaissance* (Paris 1965). A useful brief survey is his 'Recent Studies on the economic history of Venice', *Journal of Economic History* xxiii (1963). On the galley routes, see J. Sottas, *Les messageries maritimes de Venise au XIV e XV siècles* (Paris 1938), and A. Tenenti and C. Vivanti, 'Le film d'un grand système de navigation; les galères véni-tiennes XIV–XVIe siècles', *Annales: Économies, Societés, Civili-sations* xvi (1961). On coinage, see N. Papadopoli, *Le monete di Venezia* (3 vols., Venice 1893–1910), and H. E. Ives, *The Venetian Gold Ducat and its Imitations* (New York 1954). Further studies on the sixteenth-century problems are P. Sardella, *Nouvelles et speculations à Venise au début du XVI siècle* (Paris 1948), and F. Braudel, 'La vita economica di Venezia nel secolo XVI' in *La civiltà veneziana del Rinascimento* (see Section A above).

On dominion in the eastern Mediterranean and discussion of the Turkish problem, see F. Thiriet, *La Romanie vénitienne au Moyen Age* (Paris 1959), especially for the later chapters and bibliography; also F. Babinger, 'Le vicende veneziane nella lotta contro i Turchi durante il secolo XV' in *La civiltà veneziana del Quattrocento* (see Section A above). There is a more detailed study by G. Cogo, 'La guerra di Venezia contro i Turchi, 1499–1501', *Nuovo Archivio veneto* xviii (1899), xix (1900).

W. Miller, *The Latins in the Levant* (London 1908; reprinted Cambridge 1964), contains special studies of the Venetian colonies including Corfu, the Ionian Islands and the Duchy of the Archipelago. The same author's *Essays in the Latin Orient* (Cambridge 1921) contains a chapter on Crete under the Venetians. G. F. Hill, *A History of Cyprus* (4 vols., Cambridge 1940–52), includes chapters on the Venetian administration; there is a wholly inadequate, prosily romantic essay by H. F. Brown, 'Caterina Cornaro, Queen of Cyprus', in his *Studies in Venetian History* I (London 1907). On Venetian Albania, see the recent article by G. Valentini, 'Appunti sul regime degli stabilmenti veneziani in Albania nel secolo xiv e xv', *Studi veneziani* viii (1966). On Venetian Dalmatia, there is A. Tamaro, *La Vénétie Julienne et la Dalmatie* (3 vols., Rome 1918–19); an old-fashioned but enjoyable introduction is E. A. Freeman, *Sketches from the Subject and Neighbour Lands of Venice* (London 1881), and there are some interesting chapters concerning rebellion in the early sixteenth century in A. Ventura, *Nobiltà e popolo nella società veneta del '400 e del '500* (Bari 1964).

   The foreign policy and wars of Venice in Italy during the fifteenth and early sixteenth century are discussed in the works of P. Pieri, 'Intorno alla politica estera di Venezia al principio del cinquecento', reprinted in his *Scritti Vari* (Turin 1966), and *Il Rinascimento e la crisi militare italiana* (Turin 1952). See also the articles by G. Pillini, 'L'umanista Francesco Barbaro e l'origine della politica di equilibrio', *Archivio veneto* 5th ser. lxxii (1963); N. Valeri, 'Venezia nella crisi italiana del Rinascimento' in *La civiltà veneziana del Quattrocento*, and F. Chabod, 'Venezia nella politica italiana ed europea del Cinquecento' in *La civiltà veneziana del Rinascimento* (see Section A above). There are useful essays in English on the Carraresi of Padua and Carmagnola in H. F. Brown's *Studies in Venetian History* I; for Venetian involvements in the troubled period after 1494, see also J. S. C. Bridge, *A History of France from the Death of Louis XI*, vol. II (1493–98), III (1498–1507), IV (1508–14) (Oxford 1924–29). For the career of Trissino in the war of the League of

Cambrai, see E. Armstrong, 'An Italian Adventurer: an Episode in the War of the League of Cambrai', in his *Italian Studies* (London 1934).

Administrative and social consequences of mainland expansion are discussed by A. Ventura, *Nobiltà e popolo nella società veneta del '400 e del '500* (Bari 1964), which breaks new ground even though it is too ambitious, tends to sociologize and lacks a bibliography: see the reviews, by, for example, G. Cozzi in *Critica Storia* v (1966) 126–130, and by C.H. Clough, *Studi veneziani* viii (1966). Economic developments on the *terraferma* have been discussed by G. Luzzatto, 'L'economia veneziana nei secoli '400 e '500 dopo l'acquisto della terraferma', *Bergomum* xxxviii (1964); D. Beltrami, 'Beni Carraresi e proprietari veneziani', *Studi in onore di G. Luzzatto* I (Milan 1939); D. Beltrami, *La penetrazione economica dei Veneziani in terraferma . . . secoli XVI–XVIII* (Venice-Rome 1961); A. Ventura, 'Considerazioni sull'agricoltura veneta e sulle accumulazioni originarie del capitale nei secoli XV e XVI', *Studi Storici* ix (1968). There is an excellent survey by S.J. Woolf, 'Venice and the Terraferma: Problems of the change from Commercial to Landed Activities', reprinted in the volume of essays ed. B. Pullan, *Crisis and Change in the Venetian Economy in the 16th and 17th Centuries* (London 1968). Attention has also been drawn to the development of mining on the Venetian mainland in the studies by F. Braunstein, 'Les entreprises minières en Vénétie au XVIe siècle', *Mélanges d'archéologie et d'histoire de l'École française de Rome* lxxvii (2) 1965; 'Le commerce de fer à Venise au XVe siècle', *Studi veneziani* viii (1966).

III VENETIAN GOVERNMENT

Short accounts (with diagrams) of the workings of Venetian government are given by F. Thiriet, *Histoire de Venise* (see Section A above), and C.T. Davis, *The Decline of the Venetian Nobility as a Ruling Class* (Baltimore 1962). H.F. Brown, 'The Constitution of Venice and the State Archives' in his *Studies in Venetian History* I, 293–334, is a useful introduction which also discusses the judicial institutions. The fundamental study of the Venetian constitution is G. Maranini, *La costituzione di Venezia* (2 vols., Venice 1927–31); also useful are A. da Mosto, *L'Archivio di Stato di Venezia* (2 vols., Rome 1937–40); E. Besta, *Il senato veneziano* (Venice 1899). On political theory, see F. C. Lane, 'Medieval Political Ideas and the Venetian Constitution', in *Venice and History* (Baltimore 1960); G. Cozzi, 'La società veneziana in un'opera di Paolo Paruta, "Della perfectione della vita politica"', *Atti della Deputazione di Storia Patria per le Venezie* (1961). On diplomacy, see besides G. Mattingly, *Renaissance Diplomacy* (London 1955), D. E. Queller, 'Early Venetian Legislation on Ambassadors', *Travaux d'Humanisme et de la Renaissance* 88 (Geneva 1966), which contains examples of reluctance to give service. Some interesting evidence is also discussed (though mainly with reference to a later period) by B. Pullan, 'Service to the Venetian state: aspects of myth and reality in the early seventeenth century', *Studi secenteschi* v (1964).

There are short notes on each of the doges in A. da Mosto, *I Dogi di Venezia con particolare riguardo alle loro tombe* (Venice 1939), and on the problems of the early sixteenth-century dogeship there are two stimulating articles by M. Brunetti, 'Il Doge non è segno di taverna', *Nuovo Archivio veneto* new ser. xxxiii (1917), and 'Due dogi sotto inchiesta, Agostino Barbarigo e Leonardo Loredan', *Archivio veneto-tridentino* vii (1925). On prominent individual patricians there are few monographs, though for Marcantonio Barbaro see C. Yriate, *Vie d'un patricien de Venise* (Paris 1874).

IV VENETIAN CIVILIZATION

There is no comprehensive study of Venetian ecclesiastical administration and religious history. For Venetian popes, cardinals, patriarchs and bishops the basic information is in C. Eubel, *Hierarchia Catholica Medii Aevi*, vols. I–III (Münster 1898–1910), and general works on the history of the Church and the papacy should be consulted. There is a recent rehabilitation of Pietro Barbo (pope Paul II) by R. Weiss, *Un umanista veneziano, Papa Paolo II* (Venice 1958), and P. Paschini, *Il Cardinale Domenico Grimani* (Rome 1943), is useful as a short biography of a distinguished Venetian cardinal. On Gasparo Contarini, see H. Jedin, *A History of the Council of Trent* vol. I (trans. E. Graf, London 1957). Important subjects are discussed by A. Stella, 'La proprietà ecclesiastica nella Republica di Venezia dal secolo XV al XVI', *Nuova Rivista Storica* xlii (1958); G. Cracco, 'La fondazione dei canonici regolari di S. Giorgio in Alga', *Rivista di storia della Chiesa in Italia* xiii (1959); E. Pommier, 'La societé vénitienne et la réforme protestante', *Bollettino dell'Istituto di Storia della Società e dello Stato Veneziano* i (1959). On the *scuole grandi*, see P. Paoletti, *La scuola grande di San Marco* (Venice 1929); of the utmost importance is the unpublished thesis of B. Pullan, 'The service of the scuole grandi to the state and people of Venice in the sixteenth and early seventeenth centuries' (Cambridge Ph.D. 1962).

For many aspects of urban life in Venice, see Molmenti and Luzzatto (Section A above). On demographic growth, there is D. Beltrami, *Storia della popolazione di Venezia* (Padua 1954), and on building development, A. Wirobisz, 'L'attività edilizia a Venezia nel xiv e xv secolo', *Studi veneziani* vii (1965). The following should be consulted for their respective subjects: M. Newett, 'The sumptuary laws of Venice in the fourteenth and fifteenth centuries', *Historical Essays by members of Owens College, Manchester* (London 1902); C. Roth, *The Jews in Venice* (Philadelphia 1930); V. Lazzari, 'Del traffico e delle condizione degli schiavi in Venezia nei tempi di mezzo', *Miscellanea di storia italiana* i (Turin 1962); B. Pullan, 'Poverty, charity and the reason of state: some Venetian examples', *Bollettino dell'Istituto di Storia della Società e dello Stato Veneziano* ii (Venice 1960); 'The Famine in Venice and the New Poor Law', ibid. v–vi (1963–64).

On literature and humanist studies in Venice, see M. Foscarini, *Della letteratura veneziana* (2nd ed., Venice 1958); W. T. Elwert,

Studi di letteratura veneziana (Venice 1958); B. Nardi, 'Letteratura e coltura veneziana nel quattrocento' in *La civiltà veneziana del Quattrocento* (see Section A above); D.J. Geneakoplos, *Greek Scholars in Venice* (Cambridge 1962); various essays ed. V. Branca, *Umanesimo veneziano e umanesimo europeo* (Venice 1965). On printing, see H.F. Brown, *The Venetian Printing Press* (London 1891). Popular vernacular literature is discussed by A. Medin, *La storia della republica di Venezia nella Poesia* (Milan 1904). Monographs on individual scholars and literary figures include P. Gothein, *Francesco Barbaro: Fruhumanismus und Staatskunst in Venedig* (Berlin 1932); N. Carotti, 'Un politico umanista del Quattrocento: Francesco Barbaro', *Rivista storica italiana* 5th ser. ii (1937); P. Gothein, *Zaccaria Trevisan* (Venice 1942); S. Troilo, *Andrea Giuliano, Politico e Letterato* (Florence 1932); M.T. Casella and G. Pozzi, *Francesco Colonna* (2 vols., Padua 1959); V. Cian, *Un decennio nella vita di Pietro Bembo* (Turin 1885); G. Fiocco, 'Alvise Cornaro e il teatro', *Studies in the History of Architecture Presented to R. Wittkower* (London 1967).

The literature on art in Venice and the Veneto is vast; only a few titles can be given here. On sculpture and architecture, J. Ruskin, *The Stones of Venice* (London 1851–53 and subsequent eds.), must be included, and P. Paoletti, *L'Architettura e la Scultura del Rinascimento a Venezia* (2 vols., Venice 1893). Monographs on fifteenth-century architecture include: G. Boni, 'The Ca' d'Oro and its polychromatic decorations', *Transactions of the Royal Institute of British Architects* iii (1887); L. Angelini, *Le opere in Venezia di Mauro Coducci* (Milan 1945); *Le opere di Bartolomeo Bon e Guglielmo d'Alzano* (Milan 1945). T. Okey, *The Old Venetian Palaces and the Old Venetian Folk* (London 1907) is a period piece of more value than its title suggests. On 'Palladian' architecture, see J. Ackerman, *Palladio* (London 1966); R. Wittkower, *Architectural Principles in the Age of Humanism* (London 1949; 2nd ed. 1962). For sculpture, see the relevant chapters in J. Pope-Hennessy, *An Introduction to Italian Sculpture: Italian Renaissance Sculpture* (London 1958) and *Italian High Renaissance and Baroque Sculpture* (London 1963). For Donatello's work in Padua, see H. W. Janson, *The Sculpture of Donatello* (Princeton 1957). On individual painters, the following are important: V. Goloubew, *Les dessins de Jacobo Bellini* (2 vols., Brussels 1912); G. Robertson, *Giovanni Bellini* (Oxford 1968); E. Tietze-Conrat, *Mantegna* (London 1954); L. Servolini, *Jacopo de' Barbari* (Venice 1946); G. Molmenti and P. Ludwig, *The Life and Works of Vittorio Carpaccio* (London 1907); G. M. Richter, *Giorgio da Castelfranco called Giorgione* (Chicago 1937); B. Berenson, *Lorenzo Lotto* (New York 1895; revised ed. London 1956); G. Robertson, *Vincenzo Catena* (Edinburgh 1954); J. A. Crowe and G. B. Cavalcaselle, *Titian: his Life and Times* (London 1877); F. Valcanover, *Tutta la pittura di Tiziano* (Milan 1960); E. Newton, *Tintoretto* (London 1952); G. Piovene, *L'opera completa del Veronese* (Milan 1968). Connections between art and literature are discussed by F. Saxl, 'Jacopo Bellini and Mantegna as Antiquarians', in his *Lectures* (London 1957); E. Wind, *Bellini's Feast of the Gods: a Study in Venetian Humanism* (Cambridge, Mass. 1948), and most recently his *Giorgione's Tempesta with comments on Giorgione's poetic allegories* (Oxford 1969). Some suggestions about Venetian patrician patronage are made by G. Francastel, 'De Giorgione au Titien; l'artiste, le public et la commercialisation de l'œuvre d'art', *Annales: Économies, Societés, Civilisations* xv (1960).

V RECESSIONAL

Many of the titles listed above under Ch. II should be consulted, especially the volume edited by B. Pullan, *Crisis and Change in the Venetian Economy*; also F. Braudel's classic, *La Méditerranée et le monde méditerranéen à l'époque de Philippe II* (Paris 1949; 2nd ed. 1966). See also, G. Luzzatto, 'La decadenza di Venezia dopo le scoperte geografiche nella tradizione e nella realtà', *Archivio veneto* 5th ser. liv–lv (1955); A. Stella, 'La crisi

economica veneziana della seconda metà del secolo XVI',
Archivio veneto 5th ser. lviii (1956); P. Sardella, 'L'épanouisse-
ment industriel de Venise au XVIe siècle', *Annales: Économies,
Societés, Civilisations* ii (1947). On shipping, see A. Tenenti,
Cristoforo da Canal. La marine vénitienne avant Lépante (Paris
1962); *Piracy and the Decline of Venice 1585–1615* (London 1966).
The pageantry of 1571 is discussed by E.H. Gombrich,
'Celebrations in Venice of the Holy League and the Victory of
Lepanto', *Studies in Renaissance and Baroque Art Presented to
Anthony Blunt* (London 1967). Political problems of the late
sixteenth and early seventeenth centuries are analysed in A.
Stella, 'La regolazione delle pubbliche entrate e la crisi politica
veneziana del 1582', *Miscellanea R. Cessi* vol. ii (Rome 1958);
F. Seneca, *Il Doge Leonardo Donà* (Padua 1959); G. Cozzi, *Il
Doge Nicolò Contarini* (Venice-Rome 1958).

DOGES OF VENICE 1380–1580

ANDREA CONTARINI	20 January 1368–5 June 1382
MICHELE MOROSINI	10 June–15 October 1382
ANTONIO VENIER	21 October 1382–23 November 1400
MICHELE STENO	1 December 1400–26 December 1413
TOMASO MOCENIGO	7 January 1414–4 April 1423
FRANCESCO FOSCARI	15 April 1423–23 October 1457
PASQUALE MALIPIERO	30 October 1457–5 May 1462
CRISTOFORO MORO	12 May 1462–9 November 1471
NICOLÒ TRON	23 November 1471–28 July 1473
NICOLÒ MARCELLO	13 August 1473–1 December 1474

PIETRO MOCENIGO	14 December 1474–23 February 1476
ANDREA VENDRAMIN	5 March 1476–6 May 1478
GIOVANNI MOCENIGO	18 May 1478–4 November 1485
MARCO BARBARIGO	19 November 1485–14 August 1486
AGOSTINO BARBARIGO	30 August 1486–20 September 1501
LEONARDO LOREDAN	2 October 1501–22 June 1521
ANTONIO GRIMANI	6 July 1521–7 May 1523
ANDREA GRITTI	20 May 1523–28 December 1538
PIETRO LANDO	19 January 1539–9 November 1545
FRANCESCO DONÀ	24 November 1545–23 May 1553
MARCANTONIO TREVISAN	4 June 1553–31 May 1554
FRANCESCO VENIER	11 June 1554–2 June 1556
LORENZO PRIULI	14 June 1556–17 August 1559
GIROLAMO PRIULI	1 September 1559–4 November 1567
PIETRO LOREDAN	26 November 1567–3 May 1570
ALVISE MOCENIGO	11 May 1570–4 June 1577
SEBASTIANO VENIER	11 June 1577–3 March 1578
NICOLÒ DA PONTE	11 March 1578–30 July 1585

LIST OF ILLUSTRATIONS

103 *Christ before Pilate*; painting by Tintoretto, 1566–67. Photo Mansell-Anderson. Scuola di San Rocco, Venice.

104 *Miracle of St Mark freeing the slave*; painting by Tintoretto, 1584. Accademia, Venice.

105 *The mocking of Christ*; painting by Titian, *c.* 1570. Alte Pinakothek, Munich.

106 Eve; early fifteenth-century sculpture by Antonio Rizzo. Doge's palace, Venice. Photo Martin Hürlimann.

107 Adam; early fifteenth-century sculpture by Antonio Rizzo. Doge's palace, Venice. Photo Mansell Collection.

108 Nicolò Tron monument by Antonio Rizzo, begun 1476. Frari, Venice. Photo Böhm.

109 Andrea Vendramin monument by Tullio Lombardo, completed mid-1490s. S. Giovanni e Paolo, Venice. Photo Böhm.

110 Jacopo Strada; portrait by Titian, 1567–68. Kunsthistorisches Museum, Vienna.

111 Andrea Odoni; portrait by Lorenzo Lotto, 1527. Hampton Court, Royal Collection. Reproduced by gracious permission of Her Majesty the Queen.

112 Church of S. Zaccaria, Venice, by Antonio Gambella, façade by Mauro Coducci, fifteenth century. Photo Archivo Fotografico Veneziano.

113 Church of S. Michele in Isola, Venice, by Mauro Coducci, begun 1469. Photo Soprintendenza at Monumenti, Venice.

114 Ca' d'Oro, Venice, by Matteo Raverti and the brothers Buon, 1421–*c.* 1431. Photo Georgina Masson.

115 Palazzo Corner (Ca' Grande), Venice, by Jacopo Sansovino, 1532. Photo Böhm.

116 Loggia del Capitanato, Vicenza, by Andrea Palladio, 1571. Photo Soprintendenza ai Monumenti, Venice.

117 Palazzo dei Rettori, Belluno, begun 1491. Photo Soprintendenza ai Monumenti, Venice.

118 Clock-tower of the Palazzo del Capitano, Padua, ascribed to Gianmaria Falconetto. Photo Mansell Collection.

119 Porta San Tomaso, Treviso, designed by G. Bergamasco, 1518. Photo Soprintendenza ai Monumenti, Venice.

120 Porta Savonarola, Padua, designed by Gianmaria Falconetto, 1530. Photo Soprintendenza ai Monumenti, Venice.

121 *The Triumph of Scipio*; painting by Andrea Mantegna, *c.* 1504. By courtesy of the Trustees of the National Gallery, London.

122 Cloister for the canons of the Carità by Andrea Palladio, 1552. Photo Mansell Collection.

123 *Bacchus and Ariadne*; painting by Titian, 1522. By courtesy of the Trustees of the National Gallery, London.

124 *Virgin and Child enthroned with four Saints*; S. Zaccaria altarpiece by Giovanni Bellini, 1505. Photo Mansell-Anderson.

125 *St Mark enthroned*; painting by Titian, *c.* 1512. S. Maria della Salute, Venice. Photo Böhm.

126 *Feast in the House of Levi*; painting by Paolo Veronese, 1560. Louvre, Paris. Photo Giraudon.

127 Jupiter personifying Crete; detail from the relief sculptures on the *loggetta* by Jacopo Sansovino, *c.* 1540. Photo Böhm.

128 Venice as Justice; detail from the relief sculptures on the *loggetta* by Jacopo Sansovino, *c.* 1540. Photo Böhm.

129 Venus personifying Cyprus; detail from the relief sculptures on the *loggetta* by Jacopo Sansovino, *c.* 1540. Photo Böhm.

130 Justice: statue by Alessandro Vittoria above the piazzetta wall of the doge's palace, Venice, 1579.

131 Procession celebrating the Holy League; anonymous print, 1571. Correr Museum, Venice.

INDEX